A GOD ORDAINED LIFE-CHANGING 30-DAY PRAYER MANUAL WITH FASTING

ACCESSING NEW DIMENSIONS

AMOS FENWA

ACCESSING NEW DIMENSIONS

ISBN - 978-978-791-101-3

Unless otherwise indicated, all Scripture quotations in this volume are from the King James Version of the Bible.

Published by:
Amos Fenwa Ministries
156, Ikorodu Road
Onipanu Bus Stop, Lagos.
08125113314, 08033387124,
07037276477

This mini-book is designed for the annual 30-day prayer programme of HOLYGHOST CHRISTIAN CENTRE.
It is advisable to include fasting along with the prayer in order to get maximum result. You can add your own prayer point on each day of the prayer schedule.

MAY GOD ANSWER ALL YOUR PRAYERS!

- AMOS FENWA

CONTENTS

INTRODUCTION

"That Christ may dwell in your hearts through faith; that you, being rooted and grounded in love may be able to comprehend will all the saints what is the width and length and depth and height – to know the love of Christ which passes knowledge that you may be filled with all the fullness of God." Ephesians 3: 17 – 18

A popular saying that we are familiar with is "Change is the only constant thing is life". This saying is not only popular but also true. One of the relevant and consistent features of life and nature is change. Even though our God is unchangeable, everything He created was made with an in-built ability for progressive change. Due to this precious gift, man has experienced diverse depths, facets and dimensions of God's wondrous ways. From Abraham to David, Solomon to the era of the major prophets and then the minor prophets, Israel has witnessed different realms of God. Under the gospel dispensation Christ brought unmatchable changes to the world which the Apostles continued till the time of Paul. Since then we see the limitless, yet consistently faithful, demonstrations of God's power from generations to generations till date.

Seeing that God is a dimensional, limitless, unfathomable God, it is important for us to understand the many ways He expresses His diverse nature and know the price we have to pay in order to be partakers of the many dimensions of God's multidimensional nature. It is these multiple dimensions that caused the twenty – four (24) elders that were written about in the book of Revelation 4:10, to keep bowing down in worship of God because each time they looked up, they saw another dimension of God that was superior and more glorious than the one before.

There is nothing you are going through or any situation that will arise in your life that will come as a surprise to God. He has been God before time began and created us so He knows the actions each of us needs to access the change we all desire.

These principles are quite simple to grasp but the discipline needed to understand and practice them are what we need to inculcate. The new dimension of God that is necessary to enter into the change we desire will only be accessible when we apply these principles in our life.

Psychologists have said it takes 21 days to form a new habit; therefore, applying the knowledge in this book during the next 30 days will surely bring you into the new dimension of God, which will produce change for good in your life and destiny.

As you commit to partake in this 30 Days of spiritual exercise, may you experience the new dimension of God in your life.

CHAPTER ONE

WHAT IS A NEW DIMENSION?

I will start by breaking down the two key words as stated below:

NEW: produced, introduced or discovered recently or now for the first time.
DIMENSION: A level of existence or consciousness

If we combine both definitions, we can say A NEW DIMENSION is a level of existence or consciousness that is produced, introduced or discovered recently or now for the first time. This level will be higher than one experienced or known before, therefore a new dimension brings a change that is progressive and amazing in the life of the person who experiences it.

There are other definitions of a new dimension and we will consider a few of them so that we can recognize the dimension that is relevant for our lives and destinies.

· A New Dimension is the expression of the divinity in human actions.

There are many experiences that are undeniably by the hand of God. The magnificence of God is put on full display in a way that magnifies the ordinary day to day efforts of men. Notice that this divinity is not expressed or experienced in isolation, it is made visible when the beneficiary takes an action. God told Moses to drop his staff before Pharaoh in Exodus 7 and when he did, Moses' staff turned to a snake. That was extraordinary but when the Egyptian magicians did the same, Moses' snake swallowed up their snakes. Remember, God didn't mention that aspect at the initial stage.

The new dimension was displayed because Moses took the action of dropping his staff as God commanded him. We must act on the instructions that God has laid in our hearts to experience a new dimension. Human action is the platform upon which the divinity can be fully displayed.

In the midst of the ordinary, the new dimension of God causes one who gains access into it, to become extraordinary. In the midst of the spectacular, the result of access to new dimensions causes the spectacular to be exceptional. The essence of God that must be experienced by the one who taps into the divinity is seen in how his or her life takes a turn for the better. Accessing a new dimension can never leave a man in the same position, level or realm he was in. When human efforts stand out, it is an expression of access into a new dimension.

- Dimensions Are Realms

New dimensions are realms of mysterious depths made available and accessible to human actions. The depths of God are inexhaustible and manifests in such diverse ways that it keeps opening up to more and more. Like the woman at the well who desired ordinary water, Christ wanted to give her the living water that she will never thirst again which means access to realms that are unending and limitless. You can never enter the depths of God and remain the same. A distinctive change that will launch you into a new dimension is always the fruit of entering into the depths of God. Anytime instructions are unearthed and obeyed, dimensions are unveiled.

- A New Dimension Releases Higher Grace.

A new dimension is operating in a better space that indicates the release of higher grace.

This fully explains how a new dimension is essential for change from one level of grace to another. When the grace of God is upon a man, such a person does not struggle in that particular area. A new dimension eliminates the struggles and introduces ease into the person's life. Grace is the power of God that delivers you from the consequences of sin and failure. Grace is when God puts mercy on overdrive as any hindrance to the change you desire will be overridden by the mercies of God. Like Apostle Paul wrote in 1 Corinthians 15:10a, *"But by the grace of God, I am what I am, and His grace toward me was not in vain"*; the grace of God propels a person into all that God has destined for him or her to be. This power is what gives man access to a new dimension for no man can access higher dimension without the grace of God.

- A New Dimension brings Fullness.

A new dimension is a journey into the fullness of your potential and inbuilt capacity.

Please note that it is a journey, not a destination, into your full potential and all that God knew you would amount to before He created you. The journey is one of discovery and excitement because when you enter into a new dimension, it reveals a new dimension within you as well that enables you to explore the possibilities released to you through Christ Jesus. He said in John 15:11 *"These things I have spoken to you, that My joy may remain in you, and that your joy may be full."* (NKJV).

A new dimension is a journey that is not limited to physical locations but also greatly impacted by spiritual atmosphere. Engaging in prayers and fasting will cause one to travel from one spiritual location to another in an unending discovery of the depths of our limitless God. This spiritual journey does not only cause us to access spiritual realms and realities, it also shows us that we were born to do more and once that is understood, new dimensions will be unlocked to us, through and within us. The chains of limitations or restrictions are broken off our minds when we access the new dimensions. We get on an adventurous ride of pushing the limits of what can possibly be achieved through change inspired by the new dimensions in God.

- A New Dimension Unveils Your Very Best.

A new dimension is the unveiling of inner beauties and abilities inside of you. Steve Jobs was reported to have gone to a monastery for three months, just meditating and trying to break the conformity that his mind had adjusted to, and when he accessed a new dimension, the Apple Franchise was birthed. You will agree that there are electronic gadgets but the Apple chain of products is distinct in operations and functionality. That level of change and impact can be achieved by you when you access the depths within God for new dimensions. There is so much deposited within us by God and these deposits are often untapped because many do not gain access into the new dimensions in God. People suddenly step into roles and responsibilities that they felt inadequate about when they breach the boundaries of normalcy and enter into new dimensions in God. Anyone who does not break into new dimensions will become stagnant and redundant. The entrance into new dimensions is like an onion where layers of it are peeled back to reveal more within. There are layers within you that are hidden in Christ and can only be revealed through seeking new dimensions in God.

- A New Dimension Is The Embracing Of Responsibility.

The dimensions that must be stepped into for change is not a free gift, it is gotten when we take responsibility for our lives and destiny. New dimensions come when we step up to the task that we have complained about over and over again. If we keep trying the same method on the same level and it has not yielded results then it means we have to search for deeper so as to get the change we desire. This search for deeper or more brings us into new dimensions for change that we may never walk in if we do not take the responsibility to do so.

CHAPTER TWO

SIGNS OF A NEW DIMENSION

Whenever something spectacular is about to happen to a man's destiny there will be signs or changes in the circumstances that trigger a supernatural occurrence. You need to be sensitive to them and these include the following:

Restlessness:

"By your sword you shall live, and you shall serve your brother; and it shall come to pass, when you become restless, that you shall break his yoke from your neck." Genesis 27:40

Restlessness is a sign that a new dimension is calling on you. Although Jacob had stolen his brother's blessings and Isaac was offering Esau counsel on how to live life as the days go by, there was a condition that could break Esau into a new dimension and that condition is called "Restlessness". If Esau grew comfortable and remained in his 'comfort zone', refusing to step out in faith for the more that could be experienced, he would never break from the yoke upon his life. However, the moment he becomes restless, the moment comfort is taken away from him, the moment he decides that 'enough is enough', that is when the yoke of stagnancy and limitations shall be broken off his life.

Do you feel restless yet? Do you desire a change for better life, new job, opportunities, relationships, and all that God has promised you? Then your restlessness is an indication that your time to enter into new dimensions of glory, righteousness, peace and joy in the Holy Ghost has come.

For example, when a person needs to use the rest room, he or she will continue to feel restlessness until a toilet is found so he or she can "ease him or herself". When you have been called into a new dimension, you will feel a state of perpetual restlessness until you step into a new dimension that releases you into the uncommon advancement that God has in store for you. Sometimes, restlessness is an energy sent by God to move you to your next level.

During this season of fasting and prayers, take advantage of unusual restlessness. Fast, pray and prophetically employ the tool of this restlessness as the key into a dimension in God. It will push you into dimensions and new levels even though it may seem uncomfortable and painful at first. Pay attention to the restlessness within your spirit, it just might be the Holy Spirit nudging you towards your next level.

Rejection and Opposition:
"Now Jericho was securely shut up because of the children of Israel; none went out and none came in." Joshua 6:1

When the children of Israel faced opposition and were rejected entry into the land of Jericho, they saw an obstruction but God saw an opportunity for a new dimension. An opportunity to do what has never been done before nor existed before often shows up in the face of rejection and opposition. We need to change our perspective towards rejection and opposition, especially from the same people or place where we have experienced acceptance or support in the past.

The Scripture says, in Romans 8:28 that all things work together for our good whether it is acceptance or rejection. Whenever what used to be beautiful and flourishing begins to turn upside down then there is a call for a new dimension. For a great thing to begin, a good thing has to come to an end so some rejections are your promotion to your new dimensions. The withdrawal of support and acceptance sponsors us to new level if we apply it in the right way. Rejection is an activator of new levels and direction is the child of rejection – what this means is that when we are rejected, it is not the time to begin to feel sorry for ourselves or sob uncontrollably, it is time to seek the face of God for the next level. It will spring out of the present state of rejection. Remember how Philip answered Nathanael concerning Jesus' early ministry, John 1:46 *"Nazareth! Can anything good come from there?" Nathanael asked. "Come and see," said Philip.* (NIV)

Frustration and Dissatisfaction:

"I cry aloud to the Lord; I lift up my voice to the Lord for mercy. I pour out my complaint; before him, I tell my trouble" Psalm 142: 1 – 2

David, through the psalms, wrote about his frustrations and dissatisfaction to God and the Lord would always present a solution that drew David into a new dimension with God until he was known as the man after God's heart. The frustration we feel, the dissatisfaction we express is a call to a new dimension in Christ. The reason for smallness is often satisfaction with one's lot in life but frustration and dissatisfaction will often cause a shift into new dimensions for an increase in all areas of our lives. You should recognize that as children of God, frustration is a proof of unused potential so whenever you feel frustrated, change the gear through prayers, fasting and cheerful giving. Use your frustration as a stepping stone to the new dimension that God has for you. Stop holding yourself in recluse just because you're frustrated; instead be in charge to redirect your steps in the path of fruitfulness and acceleration which comes when you access new dimensions.

Hunger and Passion For More:

***Mathew** 7:7 "Ask and you shall receive, seek and you shall find, knock and the door shall be open unto you".*

The level of your dimension is at the level of your hunger. The persistence with which you approach life is an indication of new dimension. The zest to do more with the opportunities that present themselves, seeing solutions where others see challenges, finding a way out of tricky situations are sure signs that your new dimension has been activated. Hunger prepares a man to journey into new dimensions. Where hunger is lacking, life is empty for where there is hunger, there is achievement. Your desire for a new level will drive you towards acting on the instructions that God has laid in your heart to do. Nonchalance, procrastination and laziness cannot bring one into a dimension that only answers to hunger.

CHAPTER THREE

THE DIMENSIONS OF THE HOLY SPIRIT

"And the Spirit of the Lord will rest on Him – the Spirit of wisdom and understanding, the Spirit of counsel and strength, the Spirit of knowledge and of the (reverential and obedient) fear of the Lord." Isaiah 11:2 (AMP)

The call for a new dimension is not random prayer but an intentional advancement into a change of level, status and spiritual understanding. As individuals differ, so does the dimension that we desire good things differ. The Lord is able to fulfill any upgrade to new dimension, irrespective of how distinct one person's own may be from another person. To further buttress this point that there are different dimensions within the Holy Spirit, we will consider these dimensions of Holy Spirit.

- **The Spirit of Lord:**

The Spirit of the Lord upon a man changes his rank from ordinary to extraordinary. As written in the bible, the spirit of the Lord came upon David after he was anointed and transformed him from ordinary shepherd boy to the next king of Israel (1 Samuel 16:13). When we enter into this dimension, we begin to produce evidence of the presence of God because the Spirit of the Lord bears witness that Christ is the Son of God. We live in the fullness of who God has called us to be when we encounter this dimension of the Holy Spirit. Our lives are imparted with dominion and authority in such a significant way that our career, relationships, finances, family and all sphere of life reflect this dimension.

This dimension of the operation of the Holy Spirit is one that puts a man in charge. One who has entered into the depths of this dimension of the Holy Spirit manifests a supernatural realm expressed in the way they begin to exercise control and leadership in their environment. The Spirit of the Lord is the commissioning presence as we see in Luke 3:21-23 when Jesus Christ got baptized. This dimension of the Holy Spirit is the force that propels the person who gains access into this towards their destiny in God.

· **The Spirit of Wisdom:**

"And thou shalt speak unto all that are wise hearted, whom I have filled with the spirit of wisdom, that they may make Aaron's garments to consecrate him that he may minister unto me in the priest's office." Exodus 28:3

The spirit of wisdom distinguishes one from confusion or delayed obedience due to lack of clarity. This dimension of the Holy Spirit will fill the benefactor with wisdom that brings solution and success in whatever sphere they find themselves in. Access to this dimension helps a person to align with God's kingdom agenda for their generation so that they make decrees and declarations that bring an end to longstanding issues and challenges. The impartation of the Spirit of wisdom heightens our supernatural sensitivity to the times and seasons like the sons of Issachar as written in 1 Chronicles 12:32.

The spirit of wisdom is an impartation of access to divine plans and purpose for one's life. Being blessed with this dimension of the Holy Spirit will give access to answers and solutions for generational challenges. The Spirit of wisdom uncovers mysteries that will yield strategic secrets for success and produce mind-blowing transformation to the glory of God and the good of humanity.

"And Pharaoh said unto his servants, Can we find such a one as this is, a man in whom the Spirit of God is?" Genesis 41: 39

The wisdom exhibited by Joseph in translating Pharaoh's dreams was credited to the Spirit of God which is the Holy Spirit. This dimension is one that can bring industry solutions and end to global crises. Also this impartation distinguishes kings and world leaders making them to be very outstanding like King Solomon.

- **The Spirit of Understanding:**

"But there is a spirit in man: and the inspiration of the Almighty giveth them understanding. "Job 32:8

We often mistake the importance of understanding as we gather knowledge and information. The ability to comprehend what has been presented and draw conclusions from there is such a profound gift that can be accessed through the Holy Spirit. The Bible says in John

14:26 that the Holy Spirit teaches us all things and the essence of teaching is to give understanding of a difficult or previously unknown situation. This impartation of the Holy Spirit brings access to profound insight and taking cognizance of life's situations through godly interpretation and enlightenment.

The access to supernatural inspiration brings about uncommon intelligence and the dissecting of complexities. Most of our lives' issues would be solved if we got a clearer picture of what is going on so that we can figure out what to do to get the desired changed. The Holy Spirit houses the dimension that allows one to walk in such deep understanding which would remove any form of stagnancy or delay in life or destiny.

- **The Spirit of Counsel:**

"And the counsel of Ahithophel, which he counseled in those days, was as if a man had enquired at the oracle of God: so was all the counsel of Ahithophel both with David and with Absalom." 2 Samuel 16:23

Imagine operating in a dimension that people who encountered you compare you to an oracle of

God? The immense weight of this blessing is that people in dire situations come to rely on the advice that the Spirit of Counsel can bring. It is a fail-proof foundation of consultation and the ability to convey spirit filled solutions to anyone who lacks clarity. This impartation produces winning advice and ideas in a productive way by the Holy Spirit.

The Spirit of Counsel is a dimension where a step by step process of how to get from one point of destiny to another is delivered within your spirit when you access it. This dimension is the secret of uncommon advancement in life and destiny. In the end the divinely orchestrated guidance and direction received is always profitable. Accessing this dimension of the Spirit of Counsel will cause a person to be sought after like Ahithophel whose counsel was as if one spoke to God directly. This dimension of the Holy Spirit makes a person appear like they have the ears of God and sitting in the council of elders because of how accurate the counsel provided is.

- **The Spirit of Might:**

"So Samson went down to Timnah with his father

andmother, and came to the vineyards of Timnah. Now to his surprise, a young lion came roaring against him. And the Spirit of the Lord came mightily upon him, and he tore the lion apart as one would have torn apart a young goat, though he had nothing in his hand. But he did not tell his father or mother what he has done" Judges 14:5 – 6

The might exhibited by Samson during his lifetime was extraordinary yet we see consistently that it only came to play after the Spirit of the Lord came upon him. This dimension that Samson operated in effortlessly is the dimension of the Spirit of Might. This is a supernatural impartation of energy that defies weariness and tiredness. This dimension is the force of being unstoppable in the pursuits of God's revealed agenda for our lives and destiny. The doggedness with which a person keeps going in spite of insurmountable challenges is the expression of this dimension of the Holy Spirit. This energy is what pushes us to perform the action that is the ingredient added to faith to produce a change of level in life and destiny.

When the Prophet Isaiah wrote about strength in Isaiah 40:31, that makes one mount up on wings like eagles, run and not be weary, walk and not faint; he was writing about this dimension of the Holy Spirit which produces continuous and progressive victories in life. I mean the kind of might that conquers territories and bring kingdoms into submission in the kingdom of our God. Many of us have been given assignment to turn around the corruption and dearth in our industries, this dimension is what we require to fulfill the assignment in the face of many physical and spiritual adversaries. For the Spirit of Might upon a person reveals the impartation of supernatural strength and energy. Wherever the Spirit of Might is at work, destinies can never be buried by lethargy or slothfulness. Accessing this dimension causes you to wake up each day with a renewed vigor to do all that God empowers you to do, to break the hold of procrastination and step into a season of productivity.

- **The Spirit of Knowledge:**

"That the God of our Lord Jesus Christ, the Father of glory, may give to you the spirit of wisdom and revelation in the knowledge of Him." Ephesians 1:17

The beauty about the gift of prophecy is how

accurate the prophet is when we hear him or her speak things concerning our lives that they had no way of knowing. The Spirit of knowledge is such a beautiful gift that causes one to operate in such depth of knowledge and revelation that studying of books cannot give. It is an impartation by the Holy Spirit that imprints knowledge and an awareness that is beyond scope of education or literary prowess. This dimension grants the beneficiary access to inside information that opens up to the heart. When you gain access to this dimension, you begin to receive information directly from the Holy Ghost and walk in knowledge that transcends time and location. You know that you have never gone to a place or see a thing neither did you read about an event, yet the Spirit of Knowledge will cause you to describe in details what has transpired as if you were there. This dimension floods your heart with so much light that you begin to know things and hidden mysteries are revealed to you for your next level in life and destiny.

Many years ago, my wife and I were preparing to go to the embassy for an interview when I suddenly felt the nudge to ask her to put on a pink shirt. She was taken aback because I would not normally tell her what to wear, yet my wife wore the shirt and we went to the embassy. The lady who interviewed us commented on my wife's beautiful shirt and told us that pink was her favorite colour. The Spirit of Knowledge released the information that caused us to receive favour in a manner that we could not have predicted. You may wonder how the colour of a shirt may cause us to receive visas but only the Holy Spirit knows how much the colour meant to the lady who interviewed us and it brought us favour in such a spectacular way.

Many of you may have experienced situations like this when you say; "My mind told me to do this or that" and when you did it, you got expected results. That is the dimension of the Holy Spirit which by the Spirit of Knowledge provided you with information, codes and required key to enter into a new level. Delving into this dimension will grant you information for favour that will bring you into the next level in areas of your life which has been dormant.

- **The Spirit of the Fear of the Lord:**

Proverbs 14:27 *"The fear of the Lord is a fountain of life, to turn one away from the snares of death."*

This impartation deposits reverence, respect and value for the Almighty within the one who gains access to it. It is a dimension of the Holy Spirit that causes you to place God in the most valuable and highest place in your life. Your life begins to reflect the true essence of creation – to worship and adore the Lord God, Almighty. No matter how dire the situation or challenges of life may be, this dimension will cause there to always be a reason to glorify God. Impartation of this dimension opens the intuition of the bearer to seek God and His glory in every situation of life.

Like Joseph said in Genesis 39:9, access to the spirit of the fear of God will convict you in the face of acts of pleasure that dishonour God so that you may say, *"I cannot do this evil thing and sin against my God"*. Everything done in this dimension is to glorify and please God. Where the fear of God is, it becomes easier to experience the expressions of the divinity of God. This dimension is one where the presence of God will always be felt because the fear of the Lord encourages righteousness. And His presence in turn creates an atmosphere that is conducive for the wonders of God to be displayed. The Spirit of the Fear of the Lord places God on display in such a way that the glory of God is evident in the life of the person who operates in this dimension of the Holy Spirit.

The Spirit of the fear of the Lord empowers you to live in perpetual obedience to the instructions and dictates of God. Your dedication will cause a consecration that will promote God, His Kingdom and elevate you in such a powerful way that everyone who sees you will testify that you have truly been elevated into a new dimension.

- **The Spirit of Excellence:**

"Then this Daniel distinguished himself above the governors and satraps, because an excellent spirit was in him; and the king gave thought to setting him over the whole realm." Daniel 6:3

The Spirit of Excellence is one that places the inspiration of impeccable prowess in the delivery of service and/or fulfillment of responsibility and roles. The impartation in this dimension is the ability for outstanding and excellent performance. The supernatural release of life's potentials for optimal performance no matter how highly proficient the competition is.

It is a mark of outstanding delivery that is undeniably present in all spheres of live, whether spiritual, social or financial. Access into this realm by the Holy Spirit will birth a touch of perfection to rest upon anything that you do. The Spirit of excellence makes more out of the little you put efforts into doing. He teaches you how to work smartly, easily achieve the efficiency and expertise that should ordinarily take longer or more years of experience to attain.

This dimension transforms your lifestyle in such a way that it becomes impossible for mediocrity to thrive wherever you are. Your presence encourages excellence and your sight receives a keenness that points out areas that need fine-tuning and adjustments to produce uncontestable perfection. This dimension is desirable across industries and stages of life – everyone wants perfection in life and destiny – therefore access to this will surely promote advancement from one level of glory to another.

- **The Spirit of Faith**:

"Now faith is the substance of things hoped for, evidence of things not seen. For by it the elders obtained a good testimony" Hebrews 11:1 – 2

The Lord responds to our faith and more than that; the testimony, the result we desire can be attained through faith. Faith is the deed we have of the promise we have received through Christ. Many Christians do not realize what abundance we can gain access to if our faith is activated. All things are available to us through faith. Entering into the dimension of the spirit of faith is stepping into a world of abundant access. This impartation makes it easy to believe in God and take Him at His word. You take the word of God and pray with it until you get your testimony. The Spirit of Faith is the fuel that pushes one from one dimension of grace to another. It is an impartation of unshakable conviction in the irrefutable word of God and the drastic change that will bring about the possession of all the inheritance through Christ, Our Lord.

During the pandemic, where the world was shutting down and it looked impossible, we moved into Solution Arena by the grace of God and the instilling of the Spirit of Faith. When God speaks, the Spirit of Faith watches over the word till it comes to pass. When it looks like time is running out, when the pressures of life keeps mounting and when it seems like nothing is getting better, the Spirit of Faith testifies of the unchanging nature of God and His inability to lie or repent. The Spirit sustains the one who enters into the dimension as he or she attempts unbelievable feats and accomplishments.

If God has shown you a promised land, if your soul feels drained from unmet expectations and unfulfilled prophecies, step into this dimension. Your faith will be reawakened, your conviction will be strengthened and you shall see the manifestation of the promises of God for your life and destiny.

This dimension is one that equips the believers, sustains ministries and empowers the gospel of God across the world. That is why those who had gone ahead are called "FATHERS OF FAITH" for it is the Spirit of Faith that impacts longevity in ministry through the seed sown by knowledge, wisdom, might, counsel, excellence or understanding.

CHAPTER FOUR

THE DIMENSIONS OF GOD'S GRACE

"And God is able to make all grace abound toward you, that you, always having all sufficiency in all things, may have an abundance for every good work." 2 Corinthians 9:8

If God is able to make all grace abound toward us, which must mean grace is in dimensions or levels, right? Well, in God's kingdom, everything is in dimensions, measures and levels. Throughout the New Testament, the Apostles wrote about the dimensions of God's grace and it is important that we learn this too so that we do not settle only at a particular level of grace.

But first, what is grace?
Grace is the tangible evidence that a person carries the approval of God. Though unmerited, it is the mark of favour upon a life that sets him or her up for advancement in life and destiny.

With God, there is always more – to experience, to give and to receive. This understanding of the dimensions of grace also enables us to grow spiritually until we become the perfect replica of Christ on earth as He is in heaven. Many people remain on the same level of grace when they can move on to the next level because they are unaware that there are other dimensions of grace that can push a man or woman into the next level in life and destiny. So whether you operate at a great level of grace already or feel that you are just in one cadre, there is more in Christ than all humanity can exhaust. Therefore, keep knocking on the doors of dimensions in grace and you will keep going higher and higher.

These four dimensions of grace I will be highlighting below will open up the path that leads to experiencing the many dimensions that are available in Christ.

1. **Unmerited Favour**

"But God, who is rich in mercy, because of His great love with which He loved us, even when we were dead in trespasses, made us alive together with Christ (by grace you have been saved)" - Ephesians 2:4 – 5

This dimension of grace is accessible to us because of the gift of God through the death and resurrection of Christ. No one has ever been able to earn this immense love and no one can claim to deserve the grace that we all received when Jesus Christ gave Himself for our redemption. This dimension of grace is activated when we accept Christ as our Lord and Savior. When we give our lives to Christ, we do not grow taller or shorter or fatter or taller, there is no physical difference but the effect is undeniable to people we encounter. This grace is a dimension that separates the old person (sinner) from the new creation in Christ. It is an attribute of the divine love God has for all creation without discrimination. However, access to it is only granted when you believe and accept Christ as your Lord and Saviour.

It is a grace that is available for as many as would turn away from their sinful ways and come into the marvelous light of God. This grace is access to eternal life which was secured over 2000 years ago when Jesus cried, ***'It is finished'***, on the cross of Calvary. Every believer should experience unmerited favour because it is part of the inheritance we come into, when we give our lives to Christ. This new dimension is available so begin to tap into it from today onwards.

2. The Gift of cel

"But to each one of us, grace was given according to the measure of Christ's gift" - Ephesians 4:7

This gift of grace is a dimension of grace that gives us the supernatural ability to live a sanctified life. There is a dimension of grace that we step into by salvation but this new dimension is one that gives us the strength to live a righteous life on earth. This gift of grace empowers us to live in holiness and moulding us into becoming more like Christ. This dimension of grace begins the renewal of our minds by transforming our character in such a way that we begin to produce the fruits of the spirit. This grace is the sustenance for our faith and the enabling force that leads us continually into doing the desires of the spirit and not of the flesh. By this gift of grace, we are able to daily bring our bodies under submission to the will of the Lord God Almighty. Even though we live in this world, the gift of grace is the reminder, the prompt awakening of our spirit man to the truth that we are not of this world.

3. Grace for Fulfillment

"And he himself gave some to be apostles, some prophets, some evangelists, some pastors and teachers, to equip the saints for the work of ministry, to build up the body of Christ" - Ephesians 4:11

The multidimensional nature of God makes provision for all who believe they are able to walk in multidimensional grace as well. The grace for fulfillment is one that puts this diversity within the body of Christ on display. We enter into this dimension of grace when we come into alignment and agreement with God's calling upon our lives. This grace is an impartation for fulfillment of the call or ministerial office or gift of God deposited within a life.

This dimension of grace was provided to bring the church into unity with Christ. To make sure that the body of Christ will not be lacking in one area of the expression of the divine nature of God, or the other. Whether in our work place, families or relationships, the grace for fulfillment brings the beauty of our individuality to the forefront as we express the strength that has been deposited in us through this dimension of grace.

As we fully exhibit what God has bestowed upon us and show forth His glorious ability within us, we step into a dimension of God that is filled with endless possibilities and the oneness – the unity – that reveals the sufficiency with which Christians should live on this earth.

Some of us may identify our gifts early enough but for those wondering what their gift or how to fulfill the gift, this dimension of God's grace will guide you into recognizing and maximizing the call upon your life. Oftentimes, when we hear 'call of God', we immediately think it is pulpit ministry but research into the meaning of the gifts given in Ephesians 4 will show that we can fulfill our call in every facet of life, not just within the church. For example, apostles plant churches therefore a marketplace apostle will plant businesses that meet the needs of all people yet upholds the standards of God so that anyone who comes in contact with that grace will be imparted for good works.

The prophet operates in the gifts of knowledge, wisdom and counsel so a Marriage Counsellor can apply this grace to bring lasting solutions to the attack on the unity of the home using biblical principles and through the ministration of the Holy Spirit. Therefore the fulfillment of one's call in life is often rooted in their life's purpose and this grace is what pushes him or her towards a new dimension of growth and glory in life and destiny.

4. Grace for Increase

"Grace and peace be multiplied unto you through the knowledge of our Lord Jesus Christ." - 2 Peter 1:2

This dimension of grace is the one where multiplication comes upon your life. Seeing as the three dimensions of grace are being effectively utilized, this new dimension will open up because to him that is faithful in little, much more shall be given. When the unmerited favor is not abused and the gift of grace for sanctification is maximized in a life that is fulfilling the calling of God, then the grace for multiplication is the next dimension. There is increase on all levels because this dimension is an impartation of multiplication producing exponential increase on all sides.

This dimension of grace was one that Job gained access to with God where he received sevenfold restoration of all he had lost during his affliction. His faith in God was strengthened, his wealth increased, his friendship strengthened and his joy multiplied. The entrance of this new dimension is the change of level that impacts every inch of your life. Operating in this level is fundamentally based on the knowledge of God and what we can lay hold on in Christ.

In John 14:12, Jesus says we will do the works He did and do even greater than He did while on earth therefore this grace is available to us if we believe it is. This grace for multiplication brings us into an awareness of the increase that is possible through God. We become inspired to pursue God more, to love more, to give more and do all good works much more because the grace for multiplication is released upon the faithfulness we have exhibited through handling all God has blessed us with correctly.

As we can see, the other dimensions mentioned earlier are gifts from God but grace from multiplication is one that is released upon a believer with an ongoing level of intentional dedication to God and reflecting His glory through our fellowship and service. This dimension is accessed by anyone who has been stripped off all self-serving motives and truly desires to see many people experiencc life in abundance. A life of impact and dedication to God, to loving your neighbor as yourself and supporting the establishment of the Kingdom of God on earth is the code to this dimension. The beautiful thing about it is that God, through the Holy Spirit, makes this grace available to all who are willing to trust and obey.

You must already know the dimension of grace that is at work in your life now and that should be the guide for you as you pray during this period of fasting and prayers. The dimensions are not for segregation but to point to the endless possibilities of abundance that is available to us as we abide in Christ and He abides in us. No man ever walks with God and ends up empty handed. He or she is called to have more in order to be a blessing to the family and the generation he or she belongs to.

CHAPTER FIVE

DIMENSIONS OF DEDICATION TO GOD

To attain to a higher level of dedication to God in worship and service we need to have proper understanding of what it entails.

Dedication is the act of consecration and consecration is to be devoted irrevocably to God. We were created for worship – which is worship to God and for His glory – this is a duty we should not take lightly. Over the years, people wanted to know how to be more committed to God and live for Him. This dedication is a dimension that will truly cause a turnaround in your life and destiny when you begin to apply it. There are no shortcuts to living for God; it takes effort and intentionally setting aside time for the things of God. This dimension is an impartation of restoration of personal commitment to honor God with our time and resources. We see God as the owner of our souls and serve Him with the conviction that

He is indeed who He says He is.
The expressions of this dimension are as follows:

1. **Intimacy with God**

"Seek ye first the kingdom of God and his righteousness and all these things shall be added unto you." Matthew 6:33

This dimension fills you with a desire to know God for yourself. You begin to ask questions that reveal the person of God, His purpose for mankind and make His principles the guide for your life. It is an intentional and consistent fellowship that breeds spiritual growth and relationship with God. You become like the person you spend the most of your time with, why not make God that special person so that through His Holy Spirit, you can enter into the next level for your life and destiny. When you know God for yourself, you do not depend on anyone to pray for you. In fact, prophecies should confirm what God already told you during your time of personal communion. This dimension releases the ease to constantly present yourself through prayers, studying and meditating on the word of God and fasting to sharpen spiritual sensitivity that brings an awareness of who God is and who you are in Him.

The more of God you know, the more He wishes to reveal to you but you must show up to the promptings of the spirit of God calling you to fellowship. Nobody can help you to know God or pray for you like you will pray for yourself. This impartation bestows the ability to seek God, His kingdom and its righteousness so that all other things will be added unto you.

2. Service in God's House

"I was glad when they said to me, "Let us go into the house of the Lord." Psalm 122:1

This dimension is one that draws you into worship through service where you can discover and develop your spiritual gifts. It is an impartation of the joy and faithfulness that causes someone to give freely of their time and talents to the house God has planted them in. Some of the most remarkable testimonies you will experience in your walk with God will be in your place of service to Him and support for His work. This dimension opens our hearts in such a way that we grow a keen sense of responsibility and love for others like Jesus Christ, our Lord. We gain a sense of ownership for the furtherance of the gospel of God and the transformation of lives through the weekly gatherings. We do all that we find our hands to do diligently in order to ensure the smooth running of the church. We offer our talents, gifts and time to serve purpose of God in our local assembly.

This dimension is not by strength or might but by a deep desire to see the work of God continue to flourish within the church you have been planted. This is to collaborate with the overseers and elders of the church by playing your part where there are roles to be filled and responsibilities to be done. The overseers of the house of God cannot do everything; everyone's hand must be on deck for the conducting of weekly services.

As we seek this new dimension, dedication through volunteering in different church departments will promote the work of God and thereby cause our lives to also flourish. People have received opportunities for career development that turned their lives around because someone saw their dedication in the house of God. The reward of God will often meet us at the point of our service in the house of God. Commitment to support the work of God in His house – your local assembly – is a dimension that unlocks doors to advancement in life and destiny.

3. **Commitment to Kingdom Service**

"And if it seems evil to you to serve the Lord, choose for yourselves this day whom you will serve, whether the gods which your fathers served that were on the other side of the river or the gods of the Amorites, in whose land you dwell. But as for me and my house, we will serve the Lord." Joshua 24:15

Accessing new dimensions in God is also possible when we make our selves useful to the Kingdom of God. Putting it upon ourselves to do the best we can for anything that propagates the gospel of Christ and bring souls into the kingdom will surely catch the attention of heaven. This dimension is one where we willingly exist as instruments in the hands of God fit for our Master's use. This is the impartation that propels us to invest our time, money and talents into Kingdom agenda. We are fueled to be impactful people who operate as value adding agents to lives around us, including but not limited to the people of God.

This dimension calls for dedicated devotion to engaging in assignments that are dear to the heart of God. Engaging in soul winning crusades and evangelism activities in both rural and urban communities are part of the deal. To always be available to go wherever and do whatever God needs us to do becomes paramount. Getting committed to these activities will make you to be a relevant person in the fulfillment of kingdom agenda in your generation. Like Abraham, God will show you His secrets and boast about you because you have shown that you will teach your household and others within your circle of influence to walk in the path of righteousness and sustain the impact of kingdom agenda for many generations through service and giving. In this dimension in Christ, your needs will be met by supernatural supply because your dedication will cause heaven to open over your life and destiny as freely and easily as you serve God.

In summary, I will say that if God does not have to beg you to serve Him; you will not need to beg Him before He blesses you.

DAILY PRAYER SECTION

DAY 1

FLESH MUST DIE

Scripture Reading
1 Corinthians 3:3 *"For you are still carnal. For where there is envy, strife, and divisions among you, are you not carnal and behaving like mere men?"*

EXHORTATION
For God to continually bless you and for you to sustain the release of divine revelations, you must walk in the spirit. Many so-called believers are still being fully controlled by the flesh. They manifest some bad habits like *lying, pride, covetousness, lust, fornication, adultery, fraud, un-forgiveness* etc.

In this prayer program, submit to the Lord Jesus for cleansing and spiritual flushing. Let God do a thorough work in your spirit, soul and body.

CONFESSION
Psalm 51:2 "*Wash me throughly from mine iniquity, and cleanse me from my sin." (KJV)*

PRAYER POINTS

1. Lord, break me down in spirit, soul and body and re-mold me now.
2. Any habit in me hindering my full glory from manifesting, O Lord, give me grace to change it.
3. Spirit behind the works of the flesh in my life, I cast you out.
4. Lord, change me as you did for Peter and Saul.
5. Lord, show me deep revelations about heaven.
6. Let the Holy Ghost take over my life completely.
7. I shall not end my journey in carnality in Jesus' name.
8. I crucify my flesh to the cross and give way to the full expression of my spirit.
9. I refuse to be led by my flesh in my decision making process in Jesus name.
10. From henceforth, I walk by the Holy Spirit and live in the Spirit.
11. Lord, take possession of my mind and sanctify it with your power.
12. I present my body as a holy and acceptable sacrifice unto you.
13. I walk in continuous victory over the flesh.
14. I release myself to the tutelage of the Spirit.

15. Lord, guide me and carry me in your hands in this race.

DAY 2

CRUSHING THE ALTAR OF DELAY FOR GOOD THINGS

SCRIPTURE FOR THE DAY

Exodus 34:13 *"But ye shall destroy their altars, break their images, and cut down their groves."*

EXHORTATION

Many people are still waiting for the manifestation of God' s power without knowing there is an altar called delay, erected to cause the time table of the devil to operate instead of divine timing.

What is an altar?

- It is a place of contact with the spirit world
- It is a spiritual airport where spirits land and take off
- It is a place of servicing and activating Covenant
- It is a launching pad for spiritual operations.

Evil altars are raised to hinder or slow down the progress of someone or truncate the destinies of people. Balaam raised an altar to curse the children of God according to Numbers chapters 22 and 23. It is possible for someone to notice that despite his closeness to influential people, nothing works for him; this is the workings of an altar that causes delay. Whenever such a person embarks on the journey of success, something little happens on the way and he ends up in failure.

Any altar of delay raised against you to oppose the speed of God on your purpose in life and cause unending problems, prolonging affliction, shall be pulled down in the name of Jesus.

CONFESSION

Psalms 2:9 *"Thou shalt break them with a rod of iron; thou shalt dash them in pieces like a potter's vessel."*

PRAYER POINTS

1. Let the altar of delay raised against my destiny begin to collapse now in Jesus name.
2. In the name of Jesus, I shall not miss my appointed time and my appointed time will not miss me.

3. Every plan of delay against my manifestation, scatter by fire in Jesus name.
4. Network of attacks against my life generally, scatter by fire in Jesus name.
5. Anything projected or programmed into my life disturbing my hour of manifestation and visitation, come out and backfire in Jesus name.
6. Any Altar of delay crying against my manifestation, die by fire in Jesus name.
7. Any dark power extending, prolonging and elongating my season and time of manifestation, woe unto you, die by fire in Jesus name.
8. Any altar of delay, disappointment and frustration erected against my manifestation, scatter by fire in Jesus name.
9. Battles surrounding my breakthrough and manifestation come to an end in Jesus name.
10. Every strange token used to renew hardship in my life, be roasted in Jesus name.
11. Today, I separate myself from any inherited bondage and limitation, in the name of Jesus.
12. O Lord, send your axe of fire to the foundation of my life and destroy every evil

altar therein in Jesus name.

13. Blood of Jesus, flush out from my system, every inherited satanic deposit in the name of Jesus.
14. Every seed planted in my ancestry that is causing delay in my finances, family and business; catch fire in the name of Jesus.
15. I cancel the consequences of any evil local name attached to my person causing delay in my life, in the name of Jesus.

DAY 3

BREAKING EVIL ATTACHMENTS

SCRIPTURE FOR THE DAY

1 Thessalonians 2:18 *"Therefore we wanted to come to you—even I, Paul, time and again—but Satan hindered us."*

EXHORTATION

The word "attachment" means to be "joined together". When we say evil attachments, it refers to certain powers that have programmed themselves with their victims to harm and manipulate them. Paul's experience of being hindered to fulfill ministerial assignment by evil attachment is seen in the scripture above.

These evil attachments are unclean spirits that stand as a big barrier or obstacle to people's progress. All kinds of things can be attached to people spiritually such as evil spirits, demonic animals, envious witchcraft and even inanimate objects can be used to cause harm and hinder a child of God from moving to his Promised Land or place of assignment. More than an average number of people are affected by the covenant with these powers of darkness and today, per adventure you are under the influence of one, you are breaking loose right now!

CONFESSION

Isaiah 54:17 *"No weapon that is formed against thee shall prosper; and every tongue that shall rise against thee in judgment thou shalt condemn. This is the heritage of the servants of the LORD, and their righteousness is of me, saith the LORD."*

PRAYER POINTS

1. Blood of Jesus Christ, purge me of all physical

and spiritual pollutions.

2. Spiritual contaminations blocking me from having more of God; be flushed out by the blood of Jesus.
3. Yokes of my ancestors competing with the yoke of God over my life; by the anointing of the Holy Ghost, break and scatter in the name of Jesus Christ.
4. Deposits of the spirit wife/husband ministering spiritual failure in my walk with God, die by fire in the name of Jesus Christ.
5. Food eaten in dreams promoting spiritual weakness, catch fire and burn to ashes in the name of Jesus Christ.
6. Food eaten in dreams, acting as a magnet of sin in my flesh; be flushed out by fire in the name of Jesus Christ.
7. Food eaten in the physical, paralyzing my spirit man and polluting my soul; be roasted by fire and be flushed out by the blood of Jesus Christ.
8. Sex pollution in dreams, weakening my spirit; be neutralized by fire and be flushed out by the blood in the name of Jesus Christ.
9. Sexual pollution in the very act; let the blood of Jesus speak mercy for me.

10. I command all filthy corruption of the flesh to be flushed out by the blood of Jesus Christ.
11. Satanic contentions over my flesh die by fire in the name of Jesus Christ.
12. Thou law in my members, warring against the law of my mind, and bringing me into captivity to the law of sin which is in my members; break your hold in the name of Jesus Christ.
13. Every evil object attached to my glory, catch fire in Jesus name.
14. Financial losses tied to my root, I destroy you by the fire of the Holy Ghost in Jesus name.
15. O Lord, let your precious blood cleanse me from every evil attachment in Jesus name.

DAY 4

I AM CHANGING LEVELS SCRIPTURE FOR THE DAY

SCRIPTURE FOR THE DAY

Deuteronomy 1:6 *"The Lord our God spake unto us in Horeb, saying, Ye have dwelt long enough in this mountain."*

EXHORTATION

What does it mean to change a level?

1. Achieving a desired expectation regardless of current challenges.
2. It is the progressive realization of God's will in phases and stages.
3. Despising the good for the better and disregarding the better for the best.
4. The anticipation of new opportunity notwithstanding the temporary accomplishment.

You need to recognize that changing levels is God's intention for every believer because God hates stagnation. God can allow you to go around in circles so that you can learn lessons, gain experience that will take you higher in future.

Furthermore, if you lack progress people will despise you. However, it is good to realize that every change of level requires taking risks.

CONFESSION:

Proverbs 4:18 *"But the path of the just is as the shining light, that shineth more and more unto the perfect day."*

PRAYER POINTS

1. My Father, my Father; give me a word and

direction for my next level.

2. My Father, I receive power to move into the next level of my life in the name of Jesus.
3. Every satanic road-block, positioned on the way to my next level, be removed by fire.
4. Anointing to change level/status, rest upon me in the name of Jesus.
5. Every battle taken to the dream world to empty my destiny, expire by fire.
6. I break loose from every curse of untimely death this year in Jesus' name.
7. Father, let all that was stolen from me be restored this year by fire.
8. O Lord, establish me in your blessing. I am not a candidate of failure this year in Jesus' name.
9. O Lord, let your wonder working power close every door the devourer has opened in my life by fire in Jesus' name.
10. Father, move me from minimum to maximum this new quarter of the year in the name of Jesus.
11. My name shall be recommended for great things.
12. I receive every of my hanging blessings in the name of Jesus.
13. By mercy, orchestrate me to meet people

important to my next level.

14. I receive supernatural help to change my level, starting from now in Jesus name.
15. Every good thing that belongs to me in my next level shall not elude me in the name of Jesus.

DAY 5

I WILL LIVE

SCRIPTURE FOR THE DAY

Hosea 13:14 *"I will ransom them from the power of grave; I will redeem them from death: O death, I will be thy plagues; O grave, I will be thy destruction: repentance shall be hid from mine eyes."*

EXHORTATION

Every year, people die before their time because of circumstances beyond their control. So many dreams were aborted, projects unfinished, lives untouched, shed and unshed tears, broken and aching hearts. This isn't going to be your portion in the land of the living. After all, the promise of God for us is long life and God keeps His promises always! He has a track record of faithfulness. Our safety is in Jesus. We have received the life of Christ, a life that cannot be overcome by death. As a believer in Christ we possess life that is eternal. 1 Corinthians 15:26 *"The last enemy that will be destroyed is death."* (NKJV)

The bible says the devil is a roaring lion that seeks to devour. He doesn't have what we have, this is one reason why he goes about attacking the lives of God's children, oppressing them with all kinds of things and cutting lives short. But, our God is greater and is the final authority over our lives. No man has earned the right to end your life or determine how long you should live. God remains the giver of life and as you engage in the prayer points contained in this booklet, every programme of death shall be canceled over you and your loved ones in Jesus name.

CONFESSION

Psalms 118:17 *"I shall not die, but live, and declare the works of the LORD."*

PRAYER POINTS

1. I revoke now by the blood of Jesus every

sentence of death passed upon me and my loved ones by the marine, occult and witchcraft kingdom.

2. I command any sentence of death against me and my loved ones to backfire by fire in Jesus name
3. Every man or woman planning my death shall die in place of me this year.
4. I command every coffin prepared for me by my enemies to catch fire and be roasted to ashes now.
5. I command every death before my divinely appointed time to be canceled in Jesus name.
6. Let every curse of death hanging on my head be broken by the blood of Jesus.
7. I cancel every arrow of premature death in the remaining days of this year in Jesus name.
8. I command any coffin and grave that has swallowed my wealth, health, children, money, business and ministry to open and vomit them by fire.
9. I refuse to bury any of my children and loved ones this year in Jesus name.
10. I declare the release of my marriage, husband, wife and children from the cage and grave of the coffin spirit now by fire.

11. Every door of death opened before me and my family, waiting for us to walk right in, I shut you up permanently in the name of Jesus.
12. The promises of long life as spoken to me by God are established in my life and home in Jesus name.
13. The grace and power to live long is transferred to my tenth generation to come in Jesus name!
14 I shall live, succeed and do great things in the land of the living in Jesus name.
15 Every meeting held because of me, to cut my life short in its prime, is scattered in Jesus name.

DAY 6

UPROOT IT

SCRIPTURE FOR THE DAY

Matthew 15:13 "*He answered, "Every plant that my heavenly Father has not planted will be rooted up."*

EXHORTATION

Evil plantations are evil deposits planted by the devil in the foundation of men and women, these evil plantations become foundational problems. For instance, there are some people whose poverty has been planted in their foundation and no matter how educated or hardworking they are, they still end up poor.

The evil plantation in the lives of some people is untimely death. Some unfruitfulness, some marital delay and the list go on and on. The purpose of these evil plantations is to corrupt the foundation of people and the scripture talks about believers being incapacitated if the foundation is destroyed. A lot of believers today are suffering from unexplainable challenges as a result of evil plantations; however, this prayer program is designed to end it. I pray that every evil plantation in your life shall be uprooted in Jesus name.

CONFESSION

Matthew 3:10 *"And now also the axe is laid unto the root of the trees: therefore every tree which bringeth not forth good fruit is hewn down, and cast into the fire."*

PRAYER POINTS

1. I command all foundational strongmen

attached to my life to be destroyed in the name of Jesus.

2. I recover back all that plantations of darkness have stolen from me in Jesus name.
3. Every plantation of darkness in my life be uprooted by fire in Jesus name.
4. Let any rod of the wicked rising up against my family line be rendered impotent for my sake, in the name of Jesus.
5. I cancel the consequences of any evil local name attached to my person, in the name of Jesus.
6. You destructive effect of polygamy lose your hold over my life and be purged out of my foundation, in Jesus' name.
7. Every evil physical design, get out of my foundation in Jesus name.
8. You envious rivalry, get out of my foundation in Jesus name.
9. O Lord repair my spiritual foundation with your fire during this prayer program
10. Let the angel of deliverance visit me today for total transformation.
11. Lord, restore unto me all I have lost because of evil plantation.

12. Every curse hanging over my family tree, be broken this instant.
13. Anointing to disgrace my problems from the root, fall on me.
14. Any evil spirit in my foundation, release me by fire in Jesus name.
15. I receive grace to soar high in this country.

DAY 7

LIFTING MULTIPLE EMBARGOES

SCRIPTURE FOR THE DAY

1Thess 2:18 "Wherefore we would have come unto you, even I Paul, once and again; but Satan hindered us."

EXHORTATION

There was a woman in the Bible called Hannah who had an embargo upon her from bringing forth children. The Bible says her womb was shut up by the Lord. The embargo over the womb of Hannah was removed when she cried unto the Lord in prayer and with the prophetic prayer of Eli.

An embargo was laid on Shimei not to go beyond Jerusalem (1 Kings 2:36) and it led to his death.

An embargo is a restriction, limitation, a halt, a blockage, a denial, a standstill and hindrance to movement. You will know that an embargo is in place when you discover a kind of enslavement in the spirit and body. It occurs when you notice dreams of being sent on errands, for example which shows an embargo has been placed upon the progress of your life. Similarly, embargo on health can occur when there is a prolonged illness that defies spiritual and medical solutions, etc.

Embargo can come from God and from Satan. An embargo from God may be to rebuke sins as in the case of the Israelites in Nehemiah's day or bring glory to His name in the case of Hannah. When embargo comes from Satan and his agents, it is for complete destruction, stealing and killing. It is important to also know that embargoes can be self-inflicted when a person speaks evil of innocent people (Nehemiah 9:26) or rewards evil for good (Proverbs 17:13), etc.

The yoke of an established embargo can be broken by confession of sins, the exercise of spiritual violence against the embargo (Matthew 11:12) and making a covenant with God after the order of Josiah and Hezekiah (2 Chronicles 34:31).

Removing an embargo is a matter of choice, as Christ has paid the price for you to be able to do it and the joy of the salvation of the Lord shall be yours.

CONFESSION

John 8:36 *"If the son therefore shall set you free, ye shall be free indeed".*

PRAYER POINTS

1. Thank you Jesus for making provision for my deliverance by shedding your blood.
2. Confess your personal sins and that of your ancestors.
3. Every embargo placed upon my brain, I dismantle you with the thunder of God, in the name of Jesus.
4. Every embargo placed upon my glory, I dismantle you with the thunder of God, in the

name of Jesus.

5. Every embargo placed upon my destiny, be lifted now by the blood of Jesus.
6. Every embargo put upon my marital destiny, be lifted away now, by the blood of Jesus.
7. Let the thunder of God shatter to pieces every embargo of failure placed upon my life, in the name of Jesus.
8. I will triumph over all the wicked powers enforcing embargo upon my financial success, in the name of Jesus.
9. Every ministration of darkness over my life, I overthrow you now by the blood of Jesus.
10. I clear my good from spiritual warehouse in the name of Jesus.
11. I am released from the bondage of smallness in Jesus name.
12. I receive grace to thrive and flourish financially.
13. I receive unprecedented speed for every season that I have been delayed.
14. I decree my freedom today from everything contrary to the will of God for my life.
15. I decree it's my season of all round progress in Jesus name.

DAY 8

LORD SHOW ME THE SECRET OF MY LIFE

SCRIPTURE FOR THE DAY

Deuteronomy 29:29 *"The secret things belong unto the Lord our God: but those things which are revealed belong unto us and to our children for ever, that we may do all the words of this law".*

EXHORTATION

The scripture above is God's word laid bare. There are secret things and they exist in relationships, businesses, families, ministries, neighborhood, families and offices, and in every environment where a man and woman functions. There are certain examples littered all over scriptures:

Saul the King was secretly planning to kill David until the secret leaked to David through Jonathan (1 Samuel 19:1-2),Abraham knew that God would destroy Sodom and Gomorrah but the affected people did not know (Genesis 18:7-22). They were busy rollicking and junketing in their evils.

There are secret things you need to know about your foundation, neighborhood, spouse, friends, business, environment and office. There are secret things you need to know about your ministry and other engagements God planted you in. Beloved, life is not mathematics and human beings are not who you think they are.

God knows all things, including the hearts of those around you. The information of God made available to man is called revelation. You need it all the time. God has assured us in His words that He will reveal whatever we desire to know to us (1 Corinthians 2:10; Daniel 2"22; Jeremiah 33:3). All you need is to ask and wait for what God will reveal to you.

Stop assessing things on their face values— rely on God to tell you what is hidden inside the shell and as you do so, your peace and rest will stand in Jesus' name. Amen. Shalom.

CONFESSION

Daniel 2:22 "*It is He who reveals the profound and hidden things; He knows what is in the darkness, and the light dwells with Him.*"

PRAYER POINTS

Read Psalm 139:1-24 in praise of the Lord. Sing unto Him in worship.

1. God of knowledge and wisdom; glory be to your holy name in Jesus' name.
2. Open my eyes into the secret places and feed me with the information of God in Jesus' name.
3. Secret doors closed against my knowledge, open by fire in Jesus' name.
4. Holy Ghost, remove veil and evil covering over my spirit in Jesus' name.
5. Evil hands upon my eyes; wither by fire in Jesus' name.
6. Lord, show me the picture of my foundation in Jesus' name.
7. Lord, by your blood, wipe off every curse of darkness upon my spirit man in Jesus' name.
8. Spiritual cataract, die in Jesus' name.
9. Spiritual glaucoma, receive fire and die in Jesus' name.
10. Daylight darkness around my destiny, receive light of God in Jesus' name.
11. Holy Ghost, reveal to me every secret I need to know, for me to become who you want

me to be in Jesus' name.

12. Father of light, help me to sleep and wake up daily in your light in Jesus' name.
13. Lord, provide me with the wisdom needed to move my life forward after revealing the secret of my life.
14. Lord, reveal the root and source of every negative thing in my life.
15. Lord, open the eyes of my heart to behold the secrets of my life.

DAY 9

TOTAL VICTORY OVER SICKNESSES AND DISEASES

SCRIPTURE FOR THE DAY

Exodus 15:26 *"If you will diligently listen to the voice of the Lord your God, and do that which is right in his eyes, and give ear to his commandments and keep all his statutes, I will put none of the diseases on you that I put on the Egyptians, for I am the Lord, your healer."*

In the natural realm, we derive sickness from causes such as: genetics, bacteria, viruses, violating natural laws, poor lifestyle choices (i.e. diet), external trauma, stress, and psychosomatic illness as a result of emotional issues manifesting themselves physically.

In the spiritual realm, you should understand that sickness comes from the devil (Job 2:7). This cannot be left to interpretation or viewed on a case-by-case analysis. In order to overcome sickness, it is important that you know where sickness originates, in order to resist it successfully. In order to resist illness, you must submit to God. The act of submission and resistance are your personal responsibility. It is also imperative to know that Satan is aware that God's resistance is relative to your resistance. God's wish for you is to live a healthy life but as a free moral agent, you must desire the same for your life. As you fight sickness in the natural and spiritual realms, it is paramount to embrace three truths about sickness as listed below.

1. Sickness was never part of God's plan for you. (3 John 2)
2. Sickness is the work of Satan. (Job 2:7)
3. Sickness is an evil thing. (Deuteronomy 7:15)

Since sickness comes from the devil and is described in God's word as evil, we must understand that nothing good can come from sickness; it is the not-so-distant cousin of death, while life is connected to good. It is impossible to extract good (healing) from evil (sickness).

CONFESSION

Deuteronomy 7:15 "*And the LORD will take away from you all sickness, and will afflict you with none of the terrible diseases of Egypt which you have known, but will lay them on all those who hate you." (NKJV)*

PRAYER POINTS

1. Thank God for his mighty power that is able to heal all diseases and infirmities.
2. Blood of Jesus, speak deliverance unto every infirmity in my life, in the name of Jesus.
3. Every knee of disease and infirmity in my life bow in the name of Jesus.
4. Fountain of discomfort in my body, dry up now, in the name of Jesus.
5. Let the mighty healing Power of God overshadow me now, in the mighty name of Jesus.
6. I refuse to get used to ill-health, in the name of Jesus.

7. Every serpent and scorpion of affliction, die, in Jesus name.
8. O Lord, let all that has to be shaken out of my life, be shaken out, in the name of Jesus.
9. I shall see sickness no more in my body in the name of Jesus.
10. Father Lord, let the whirlwind of God scatter every vessel of infirmity and disease fashioned against my life, in the name of Jesus.
11. I denounce every engagement with the spirit of death, in the name of Jesus.
12. Holy Spirit, speak deliverance into my life, in the name of Jesus.
13. Thou Covenant of Affliction and sickness, die, in the name of Jesus.
14. I recover every organ of my body from evil altar, in the name of Jesus.
15. Blood of Jesus, flush out every evil deposit out of my blood, in the name of Jesus.

DAY 10

BREAK FORTH

SCRIPTURE FOR THE DAY

Isaiah 44:23 "*Sing, O ye heavens; for the Lord hath done it: shout, ye lower parts of the earth: break forth into singing, ye mountains, O forest, and every tree therein: for the Lord hath redeemed Jacob, and glorified himself in Israel.*"

EXHORTATION

What does it mean to break forth? It means to forcefully advance in a way that others cannot, command attention in a positive direction, move forward from the ordinary, breaking the status quo, etc.

When it is the time for a man to break forth, there is often a release of power (Acts 10:38), followed by the removal of obstacles and struggle. Then the mountains are leveled (Psalm 126:1-6) for you to step into a new dimension, new experience, new opportunities and new things that reveal another side of you, exposing your inner beauty.

It is your time to break forth in your family, amongst your peers and at your place of work.

CONFESSION

Isaiah 58:8 *"Then shall your light break forth like the dawn, and your healing shall spring up speedily; your righteousness shall go before you; the glory of the Lord shall be your rear guard."*

PRAYER POINTS

1. Every power prolonging state of stagnancy/delay in my life, die in the name of Jesus.
2. Any power prolonging poverty in my life, die in the name of Jesus.
3. Every power that wants to waste my destiny be wasted, in the name of Jesus.
4. Every arrow fired into my head to return me to square one, back fire in the name of Jesus.
5. Yoke of Kadesh-Barnea in my life, break, in the name of Jesus.
6. Every vehicle of stagnancy in my life, I knock you off today, in the name of Jesus.
7. Every stronghold, binding me to failure, frustration and backwardness, die in the name of Jesus.

8. You, power of failure, frustration and backwardness, die, in the name of Jesus.
9. Let the power to find my bearing in the journey of life come upon my life, in the name of Jesus.
10. Desert arrows fired against me, backfire, in the name of Jesus.
11. Holy Ghost fire — cut off every umbilical cord still attached to Satan in my life, in the name of Jesus.
12. Every bondage of cyclical or seasonal problems break in the name of Jesus.
13. I withdraw my name from the book of born for nothing, in the name of Jesus.
14. 1 shall get to my destination at the appointed time, in the name of Jesus.
15. I shall not take a longer journey to my inheritance, in the name of Jesus.

DAY 11

WINNING THE BATTLE OF MY LIFE

SCRIPTURE FOR THE DAY

1 Samuel 17:45-50 *"Then said David to the*

philistine, Thou comest to me with a sword, and with a spear, and with a shield: but I come to thee in the name of the LORD of hosts, the God of the armies of Israel, whom thou hast defied. This day will the Lord deliver thee into mine hand. and David went on to prevail over the philistine with a sling and with a stone, and smote the philistine, and slew him; but there was no sword in the hand of David."

EXHORTATION

There are five categories of people in life at every point. They are those who have:

- Just won a battle
- Lost a battle
- In the midst of a battle
- Entered into a battle and
- Those who seem to have no battle.

There are certain battles we need to fight, rivers we need to cross, giants we need to conquer and lions we need to kill to make life easy for our children, their children, and their generations to come. We can not allow them to continue with the oppression that has tagged since the time of our forefathers down to our parents. We need to resist and defeat them.

Some African parents obtained favors and got into evil commitments from demons or Satan and used their children or future generations as collateral or surety, e.g: success of children, health, fruitfulness, longevity through oaths, covenants, pacts, etc. and this compromised the destiny of failure generations.

CONFESSION

Jer.1:19 *"And they shall fight against thee; but they shall not prevail against thee; for I am with thee, saith the lord, to deliver thee".*

PRAYER POINTS

1. O Lord put an end to the battle of my life now in Jesus name.
2. Lord let me praise you more now than engage in fighting battles in Jesus name.
3. I command in the name of Jesus, let the battle concerning my marriage expire now.
4. I command in the name of Jesus, let the battle concerning my health expire now.
5. I command in the name of Jesus, let the battle concerning my business expire now.
6. I command in the name of Jesus, let the battle concerning my career expire now.

7. I command in the name of Jesus, let the battle over my children expire now.
8. I scatter all evil congregations and groups hired to stop the fulfillment of my prophecy.
9. I shall not die in battle as Uriah did.
10. I shall not die in battle as Samson did.
11. I receive the anointing to overcome all battles of my life.
12. I decree that I am a survivor; I will survive sickness, poverty, lack, premature death.
13. Every ancestral negative pact at work in my life, I cancel you by fire.
14. Every evil oath taken on my behalf by my parents or grandparents; I relinquish myself by the blood of Jesus, right now in Jesus name.
15. I speak and declare victory over every battle in my life in Jesus name.

DAY 12

PRAYER FOR THE NATION

SCRIPTURE FOR THE DAY

Jeremiah 29:12-14 *"Then shall ye call upon me, and ye shall go and pray unto me, and I will hearken unto you.*

And ye shall seek me, and find me, when ye shall search for me with all your heart. And I will be found of you, saith the LORD: and I will turn away your captivity, and I will gather you from all nations, and from all places wither I have driven you, saith the LORD; and I will bring you again into the place whence I caused you to be carried away captive."

EXHORTATION

The world has taken a new turn. Several laws are passed and several restrictions are being placed. The enforcement of things that are not only morally wrong but scripturally wrong is now the order of the world. In one part of the world, especially Nigeria, West Africa; there is the lackadaisical attitude of the leaders towards the people they swore to serve causing hardship for the citizens with hike in prices, massive unemployment, currency devaluation and the incessant killings of innocent lives.

Our nations are under a siege and the devil has his minions planted in almost every strata of government. In Nigeria, there is increasing insecurity and a tough battle to hold the seat of power in the forthcoming elections. To stop the devil's workings in our nation, it is imperative that we pray hard.

CONFESSION

2 Chronicles 7:14 *"If my people, which are called by my name, shall humble themselves, and pray, and seek my face, and turn from their wicked ways; then will I hear from heaven, and will forgive their sin, and will heal their land".*

PRAYER POINTS

1. Lord, let the wickedness of the wicked in this nation come to an end.
2. In the name of Jesus, we decree the enthronement of justice in all the affairs of our nation.
3. In the forthcoming elections, Lord, take absolute control.
4. We sabotage the plan of the evil ones over this nation in the forthcoming elections.
5. Lord, let there be no loss of lives and properties; by your mercies, grant us a free and fair election.
6. Lord, dispatch your angels to the four corners of this nation to stop the insecurity that besiege us.

7. By the blood of Jesus, we ransom our nation from every power that wants to destroy her destiny.
8. O Lord, visit us with a strong and powerful hand in this nation in Jesus name.
9. O God of Elijah set Nigeria free from the hand of the satanic cabals oppressing the nation.
10. By the blood of Jesus, our nation is delivered from every form of illegality.
11. We decree that our dignity is restored as a nation in Jesus name.
12. For the sake of the elect, deliver our nation from utter destruction.
13. We speak the peace of God over our nation and leaders in authority.
14. Lord, take away the heart of stone from our leaders and direct them to do your bidding.
15. Lord, usher our nation to a season of new dimensions in Jesus name.

DAY 13

THE POWER OF PROGRESS

SCRIPTURE FOR THE DAY

Exodus 14:15 *"And the Lord said unto Moses, Wherefore criest thou unto me? Speak unto the children of Israel, that they go forward:"*

EXHORTATION

God's desire is that we keep marching forward. It is not a crime to start small, but it is definitely a crime to get stuck there. Every Christian must join the progressive 'party' of God. Do you want to become an overtaker? Then, you need to progress. What is progress? Progress is advancement that is measurable. You must progress and the reasons are:

- God commands and desires your progress.
- To shame your adversaries and be a change agent.

There are factors that hinder people's progress, such as:

- Enemies of progress: It is expedient to keep your circle small, if you want to travel far, travel light.

- Secret sins
- Laziness and indolence
- Impatience with God etc.

You need progress spiritually, mentally and in your financial life and every facet of life.

CONFESSION

Proverbs 4:18 *"But the path of the righteous is like the light of dawn, that shines brighter and brighter until the full day."*

PRAYER POINTS

1. Anointing to progress this year, fall upon me, in the name of Jesus.
2. Every dark power holding night vigils against my progress, be destroyed in the name of Jesus
3. Every power making it difficult for me to progress; vanishe in the name of Jesus.
4. Every power making it difficult for my business to progress, vanish, in the name of Jesus.
5. Every power disturbing my progress I announce your obituary; die, in the name of Jesus.

6. Every strange wind blowing against my progress, stop now, in the name of Jesus.
7. Every door of progress I have been knocking over the years, open now, in the name of Jesus.
8. Every bar of limitation on my progress, scatter by fire, in the name of Jesus.
9. Mantle of divine progress, fall on me in the name of Jesus.
10. Anointing for speedy progress, fall on me, in the name of Jesus.
11. Any Red Sea between me and my progress, part for me to go through, in the name of Jesus.
12. Every Pharaoh (stubborn enemy) pursuing me relentlessly, give up and die in the name of Jesus.
13. Every power manipulating my speed in life, expire in the name of Jesus.
14. From henceforth, the path of my family, business and finance shall shine brighter and brighter.
15. I walk into open doors in Jesus name.

DAY 14

IT'S MY SEASON OF UNPRECEDENTED FAVOUR

SCRIPTURE FOR THE DAY

Exodus 12:36 *"And the LORD gave the people favor in the sight of the Egyptians, so that they lent unto them such things as they required. And they spoiled the Egyptians."*

EXHORTATION

The word 'unprecedented' means 'an occurrence never seen before' or something that has not happened before. So, unprecedented favour means the kind of favour that has never been seen before. God has been in the business of bestowing favour upon people, it didn't just start today. From the scripture for the day, we see this same favour come upon the children of Israel when they were about to leave Egypt. They were slaves to the Egyptians who hated them, yet when God gave them favour, the Egyptians had no option but to respond accordingly and this was instrumental to how they left Egypt with lots of gold, silver and raiment (Vs 35). It was indeed unprecedented; an example of the things that only

God can do.

This same unprecedented favor came upon Esther when the King was looking for a woman to replace Queen Vashti. Esther with the Jewish name Hadassah was forced into exile in that foreign land and despised, therefore, the thought of being accepted as a queen was unthinkable. When God decided to favour her, the impossible became possible; a Jewish orphan became the queen of the land. Your story will change too.

CONFESSION

Psalm 90:17" *Let the favor of the Lord our God be upon us, and establish the work of our hands upon us; yes, establish the work of our hands!"*

PRAYER POINTS

1. Lord, let me be at the right place at the right time in Jesus name.
2. Let people come from north, east, west and south to pick me; none but only me!
3. As a result of the favour of God, my request will be granted speedily in Jesus' name.
4. The remaining months this year, I will

experience unprecedented results in Jesus' name!

5. Let favour bring to me amazing successes and accomplishments in Jesus' name!
6. The kind of favour that will not make me not go empty-handed in my job, career, business, marriage; I receive it in Jesus' name!
7. I declare that I will enjoy God's goodwill in all spheres of my life henceforth.
8. Whatever is killing my neighbors or people around me will not kill me in Jesus' name
9. It takes an established person (like David) to establish another (like Mephibosheth). God's favor will establish me in Jesus' name.
10. It doesn't matter if people like or think I'm not good-looking enough, God will position me to be blessed even by my adversaries in Jesus' name
11. Even when others see me as unqualified, God will favour me in Jesus' name.
12. The place where my location and position will be upgraded; let them begin to be remember me from today in Jesus' name.
13. Upon my arrival to any office where I seek approval, I shall find favour in Jesus' name.
14. The God that changed Saul to Paul will change

my destiny for the better in Jesus' name.
15. Let favour reign in my life today and forever in the name of Jesus.

DAY 15

COVENANT DAY OF MIRACLE MARRIAGE

This is the day to pray in unity for the Singles (Bachelors & Spinsters) among us. Nearly every family has one or two people believing God for marital settlement as this day is set aside to intercede for them for marital joy.

NONE SHALL LACK HER MATE

SCRIPTURE FOR THE DAY

Isaiah 34:15&16 *"The owl will nest there and lay eggs, she will hatch them, and care for her young under the shadow of her wings; there also the falcons will gather, each with its mate. Look in the scroll of the LORD and read: None of these will be missing, not one will lack her mate. For it is his mouth that has given the order, and his Spirit will gather them together."*

EXHORTATION

Adulthood is not just a function of age; rather, it is an attainment and serves as a form of achievement. Throughout human history, young people have aspired to attain adulthood and have worked hard to get there. The three nearly universal marks of adulthood in human societies include marriage, financial independence, and readiness for parenthood. Now, the very concept of adulthood is in jeopardy.

Study after study reveals that young people are achieving adulthood, if at all, far later than previous generations are now living. In America, the average age of marriage for young Americans, fifty years ago, was in the very early twenties. Now, it is trending closer to age thirty which is tagged the "stigma" age for an unmarried female in Africa.

Why is this important to us all? A stable and functional culture requires the establishment of stable marriages and the nurturing of families. Without a healthy marriage and family life as foundation, no lasting and healthy community can long survive. Hence, the need to get settled in adulthood and marriage early for a thriving family that will in turn make healthy communities, states, countries and the world at large. We cannot give any chances to delay.

These prayer points are to deal with delay in marriage.

CONFESSION

John 16:24 "*Hitherto have ye asked nothing in my name: ask, and ye shall receive, that your joy may be full*".

PRAYER POINTS

1. Thou power of error in choosing the right partner be disgraced in the name of Jesus.
2. My divine partner! Wherever you are, manifest and locate me by fire in Jesus name.
3. The strongman in charge of marital failure in my family, be exposed, disgraced, and die by fire in the name of Jesus.
4. Anointing of the Holy Ghost! Break every yoke of failure attached to my marital destiny in the name of Jesus.
5. I break every covenant of marital failure and late marriage in the name of Jesus
6. I cancel every spiritual wedding conducted

consciously or unconsciously on my behalf in Jesus name.

7. Household powers stopping me from meeting my life partner die in Jesus name.
8. The evil veil blocking my God-ordained partner and I from noticing and attracting each other, catch fire and burn to ashes.
9. Every magnet that is drawing me and my God-ordained partner farther from each other be shattered into fragmented pieces in Jesus name.
10. Evil program designed against my marital destiny, be deprogrammed in the name of Jesus!
11. Every evil authority over my marital life be scattered in the name of Jesus.
12. I break every curse and covenant of loneliness by the blood of Jesus.
13. Lord let there be open doors financially for my spouse in Jesus name.
14. As I wait for your promise, O Lord, uphold me with Your right hand.
15. Lord, direct my relationship and let it bring you glory in Jesus name.

DAY 16

LORD I NEED YOUR INTERVENTION

SCRIPTURE FOR THE DAY

Daniel 6:21-22 *"Then said Daniel unto the king, O king, live forever. My God hath sent his angel, and hath shut the lions' mouths, that they have not hurt me: forasmuch as before him innocence was found in me; and also before thee, O king, have I done no hurt".*

EXHORTATION

There are occasions in every man's life when he finds it difficult to receive help and no one wants to help. David said *"when my father and mother forsake me then the Lord will take me up"*. In other words, our fathers and mothers might forsake us. And, there are occasions when those who want to help may fail. The scripture talks about the possibility for a woman to forget her sucking child and in comparison to God's inability to fail those who rely on Him for help.

There are occasions when it is beyond the ability of man to help. But, the Almighty God said "W*hen you pass through the rivers I will be with you, when you pass* *through the water it won't overflow you and when you pass through fire, it will not burn you because I will be there by your side!"* Now there is no friend who will pass through the fire with you.

In all of these cases, it is clear that what we need is divine intervention. I am certain that for everyone who desires His intervention, He will intervene. With Him, all things are possible.

CONFESSION

Psalm 20:1-2 "May the Lord answer you when you are in distress; may the name of the God of Jacob protect you. May he send you help from the sanctuary and grant you support from Zion."

PRAYER POINTS

1. Lord, have mercy on me.
2. Father, you are the Great Physician, do what the doctors cannot do concerning my health.
3. O God, intervene in my financial life! I don't want to die poor. I am tired of managing!
4. Father, wherever my blessings may be hiding – east, west, north or south; send your angels tonight, let them bring in my blessings.

5. Father, I want to be fruitful. Intervene in every area of my life that is barren.
6. Lord, intervene in the lives of the Singles who are of marriageable age, young widows, young widowers and single mothers; may they get married this year.
7. Every wall of Jericho that the enemy has built around me, O Lord, pull it down in Jesus name.
8. O God of intervention, arise and break away every chain that has tied me to where I don't like in Jesus name.
9. By your intervention, O Lord let all my delayed miracles and achievements manifest now in Jesus.
10. O Lord, divinely orchestrate my steps to meet the right people for my next level.
11. Father Lord, pull me out of whatever dark place I am in, right now.
12. O Lord, let your perfect will be revealed in my life in Jesus name.
13. My Lord, give me the wisdom required in my finances.
14. O Lord, enlarge my coast in Jesus' name.
15. Father Lord, arise in your anger and fight against those who plot against me.

DAY 17

HELP FOR MY ASSIGNMENT

SCRIPTURE FOR THE DAY

Ephesians 2:10 *'For we are his workmanship, created in Christ Jesus for good works, which God prepared beforehand, that we should walk in them."*

EXHORTATION

An assignment is a mission or position to which a person is assigned. We all have a distinct mission to fulfill here on earth; and to get fulfilled, we need help. God has a divine assignment for each Christian. Your assignment is any problem that you were created to solve. These problems are also your doors to rewards. This is where favour comes in. But how do you recognize your divine assignment? God has already placed a specific assignment in your life that only you can accomplish with His help. Everybody in life needs a helper at one point or the other in the journey of life.

You cannot afford to be a lone-ranger on earth; your life is interwoven with other lives, absence of which causes delay, pains and frustration. There are people that have been positioned by heaven to make the journey of your life smooth and if you miss these sets of people, your life becomes unproductive. It is God that helps, he is the source of all help; however, he makes use of men as machinery for the delivery of these help on earth.

PRAYER POINTS

1. Every veil of darkness, covering my destiny helper from locating me, be removed in Jesus name.
2. Every visible and invisible force assigned to hinder my connection with my destiny helpers, be arrested in Jesus name.
3. Heavenly Father, break every wall of partition between me and everyone assigned to lift up my head in Jesus name.
4. By the fire of God, I break every covenant of promise and fail operating in my life in Jesus name.
5. Every spirit of antagonism on assignment to deny me of due help, be destroyed in Jesus name.
6. By the force of favour, speedily connect me with my destiny helpers in Jesus name.

7. Father, frustrate the counsel of evil over my life assignment in the name of Jesus.
8. Every of my destiny helper that has been held down in the prison of life, be released speedily by the fire of the Holy Ghost and locate me in Jesus name.
9. Heavenly father, by divine set up, arrange a meeting between me and my destiny helper that will lead to my change of story this season in Jesus name.
10. Oh Lord, in the order of Mordecai, arrange my remembrance in the heart of everyone that has been heavenly ordained to help me in Jesus name.
11. I decree my help has come this day in Jesus name.
12. I attract help from all corners of the earth.
13. I decree that helpers would arise to me daily in Jesus name.
14. From today O Lord, position me never to miss my helpers in Jesus name.
15. I banish every anti-help spirit at work in my life right now, in Jesus name.

DAY 18

LET MY FINANCIAL GATES OPEN

SCRIPTURE FOR THE DAY

Isaiah 60:11 *"Therefore thy gates shall be open continually; they shall not be shut day nor night; that men may bring unto thee the forces of the Gentiles, and that their kings may be brought."*

EXHORTATION

Gates are very important. Just as in the natural realm where gates are used for security and protection, God uses spiritual gates which you can't see with your physical eyes like you can see the gate of your house, church, or office, to secure, protect and fortify people's lives.

You must know that the devil also has spiritual gates in effective operation, you can't see them but they are real. These evil spiritual gates existed in the time of Abraham and other Bible characters (**Genesis 22:17**) and they still exist today. Gates also serve as entry points to a house (**Luke 16:20**), city (**1 Kings 17:10**), palace (**Esther 5:13**), church (**Acts 3:2**), or a person's life (**Isaiah 60:11**). While

God has gates He uses to pass or release blessings and good things into our lives, the devil uses his own evil gates to pass or introduce sin, problems, afflictions and all manner of evil into people's lives.

God promised us in Isaiah 45:2-3 saying "*I will go before you and make the crooked places straight, I will break in pieces the gates of bronze and cut the bars of iron; I will give you the treasures of darkness and hidden riches of secret places, that you know that I, the Lord, who call you by your name, am the God of Israel.*"

God needs to clear the way for you to be able to take delivery of the treasures of darkness and hidden riches of the secret place; until the gates of brass are pulled down, there will not be any secret riches.

CONFESSION

Revelation 3:7 "*Write this to Philadelphia, to the Angel of the church. The Holy, the True—David's key in his hand, opening doors no one can lock, locking doors no one can open—speaks.*" (MSG)

PRAYER POINTS

1. Let my gates of divine blessings open in Jesus name.
2. Let the power to enter through my gates of blessings come upon me now in Jesus name.
3. You strong man standing at the gates of my destiny, fall down and die in Jesus name.
4. Evil monitors at the entrance of my gates of blessing, scatter now in Jesus name.
5. O Lord, shatter to pieces every gate of bronze; every gate of stagnation erected around my life.
6. O Lord, my Father, cut asunder, cut down all bars of iron hindering and resisting my spiritual, financial, career, educational, marital progress.
7. I declare immediate manifestation of all round progress into my life.
8. Father in the name of Jesus Christ, I destroy whatsoever that is used spiritually or physically to shut my door by fire in Jesus Name. (Joshua 6:1)
9. Father in the name of Jesus Christ, every spirit of dryness and closure that has besieged my financial open door to bring me to emptiness; I destroy you now by the power of the blood

of Jesus Christ. 2 Kings 6: 24-25

10. Father, make me a pillar of support to help in the expansion and growth of the church.
11. Lord, open every closed door against my finances.
12. Lord, approve my name to be mentioned for favour in places that matter.
13. I receive the grace to step into financial favour from today.
14. Lord, in times of economic recession, I will enjoy your abundant provision in Jesus name.
15. I decree and declare that my finances will not sink in Jesus name.

DAY 19

HEAVEN CONSCIOUSNESS

SCRIPTURE FOR THE DAY

1 Corinthians 15:19 *"If all our hope is just in this world, we are among men most miserable."*

EXHORTATION

It is expedient to know that you are an eternal being, made in the likeness of God (Genesis 1:27).

Your time here is short; hence, do not be carried away by the cares of this world. You should live in the present with the end in mind; being heaven conscious, knowing that you will give account for everything that you do on this earth.Our Lord is coming back again and every believer – you and I – are to stay ready. The renewal of our minds cannot be over-emphasized; the fervency to watch and pray must be fanned to flames. The consistency of our fasting and prayer is needed so that we can put our flesh under subjection to the Spirit and not miss the clarion call on that fateful day.

CONFESSION

Jude 1:24 *"To him who is able to keep you from stumbling and to present you before his glorious presence without fault and with great joy."*

PRAYER POINTS

1. Thank you Lord for the gift of eternal life.
2. Lord, teach my heart to love and serve you all the days of my life.
3. I bring down everything that exalts itself against God in my heart and I enthrone God as the King over my life.
4. Lord, search my heart for whatever doesn't

look like you and purge it in Jesus name.

5. Lord, forgive me of every sin that may stand against me on the Day of Judgment.
6. Lord, continue to keep me in your perfect will.
7. Empower me O Lord to preach the gospel according to your divine mandate.
8. Lord, continue to lead me on the path of righteousness
9. Lord, work on my eyes and heart to remain fixed on you at all times.
10. I pray that the eyes of my understanding become enlightened to know the hope of your calling.
11. I take away every distraction in me and look unto Jesus, the Author and Finisher of my faith.
12. Lord, help me to be bold about salvation so that unbelievers can also take part of it.
13. Lord, as you have saved me, show mercy to every member of my family and write our names in the Book of life.
14. The forces that derailed Demas will not succeed against me and my household.
15. In this race of righteousness, I will not fail nor faint in Jesus name.

DAY 20

NOT MY BLOOD

SCRIPTURE FOR THE DAY

1 Samuel 26:20 *"Now do not let my blood fall to the ground far from the presence of the LORD. The king of Israel has come out to look for a flea—as one hunts a partridge in the mountains."*

EXHORTATION

There is a war going on spiritually, every minute and day. Satan has his agents strategically positioned in different places of the world to make sure that the will and agenda of God does not stand on earth. Therefore, the believer needs to be alert to defend his territory and fight back the beast - the enemy called Satan.

For example, in Nigeria, West Africa, the election period is a time for bloodshed by those who are power drunk and want to get into the seat of power at all cost. The assignment of the enemy is to waste people in this season but I hear God saying to tell you "NOT MY BLOOD."

Longevity is our covenant right. God spoke to Abraham in Genesis 15:15 saying, *"Now as for you, you shall go to your fathers in peace; you shall be buried at a good old age."* We are connected to Abraham through the birth and death of Jesus Christ and are redeemed by the blood of Jesus. Covenant of redemption qualifies us for long life in Christ Jesus and so, our blood will not be used by the devil and his minions.

CONFESSION

Revelations 12:11 *"And they have conquered him by the blood of the Lamb and by the word of their testimony."*

PRAYER POINT

1. Blood of Jesus! Erase my name from the list of those marked for death this year.
2. God that answers by fire! Arise and make it impossible for enemies to spill my blood this year.
3. Anyone dragging me to an evil altar for slaughter; fall down and die in my place.
4. Anyone drinking the blood of my marriage, business and ministry, die by fire.
5. Blood of Jesus! Arise! Raise up a standard against those who rise up against me to drink

my blood.

6. Hunters of my soul; the blood of Jesus shall contend against you for my sake.
7. You this ground! In the name of Jesus, I declare that you shall not drink my blood this year.
8. Drinkers of blood and eaters of flesh in my family; your time is up, receive the judgment of fire.
9. I refuse to be donated by witchcraft agents operating in my family.
10. Any blood sucking well that has been prepared for me to fall into, I bury it in the name of Jesus.
11. I nullify and go against any blood sucking covenant organized in the dark kingdom to kill me before my time.
12. Every plan to use my blood as an ink to sign their demonic document, I erase it by the blood of Jesus.
13. I escape every trap of the enemy to have my blood in the name of Jesus.
14. I declare that every territorial place marked for the drinking of blood will have no effect on me and my family in Jesus name.
15. My family and I are covered by the blood of Jesus.

DAY 21

COVENANT DAY OF FRUITFULNESS

(Today is set aside to intercede for those waiting for miracle babies amongst us and within our friends and family)

SCRIPTURE FOR THE DAY

Genesis 25:21 *"And Isaac intreated the Lord for his wife, because she was barren: and the Lord was intreated of him, and Rebekah his wife conceived."*

EXHORTATION

Marriage is a beautiful thing and although it is not a smooth journey and the couple would navigate through life together in tough seasons, grow with each other and learn to accept their differences, God does not wish that any marriage should go through the pain of unfruitfulness. God said to the man after He had created Him "be fruitful and multiply" (Gen.1:28), this is what God still expects till date.

However, the major challenge for many women in marriage is the delay in bearing children, characterized with the fear of reaching menopause or having just one child.

Prayers can cause a barren woman to bear children. I find praying the word of God as a solution for putting an end to the era of unfruitfulness in marriage - whether the marriage be under a curse or it is by natural causes. I see God changing the stories of many women through today's prayers.

CONFESSION

Psalm 127:3-5 *"Lo children are an heritage of the Lord: and the fruit of the womb is His reward. As arrows are in the hands of a mighty man; so are children of the youth. Happy is the man that hath his quiver full of them: they shall not be ashamed, but they shall speak with the enemies in the gate."*

PRAYER POINTS

1. I stand by your word in Genesis 1:28 today and I declare that I am fruitful in Jesus name.
2. Under the new covenant, Jesus paid the price for my fruitfulness; therefore, I receive my children today in Jesus name.
3. I uproot whatever seed has been sown to cause

my barrenness today.

4. For with you, nothing is impossible, so I declare that I shall be pregnant and deliver my baby this year in Jesus name.
5. My womb; hear the word of the Lord through me, be opened and carry my children in Jesus name.
6. From today, I am no longer called a barren woman but a mother of many children.
7. O Lord, reveal to me the solution to my unfruitfulness in Jesus name.
8. I nail to the cross, the grief that I feel over barrenness in Jesus name.
9. I declare that there shall be no more miscarriages in my life.
10. Lord, remember me as you remembered Rebecca, Rachel and Hannah.
11. Lord, cause my womb to be fertile in Jesus name.
12. Lord, I receive your mercy today.
13. I declare over my soon-to-be born children, they will serve the Lord and bring joy to me.
14. Lord, let my appointed time for conception come.
15. Let every attack of the enemy fighting my reproductive organs begin to back fire now!

Day 22

GRACE FOR CELEBRATION

SCRIPTURE FOR THE DAY

Esther 9:20-22 *"As the days wherein the Jews rested from their enemies, and the month which was turned unto them from sorrow to joy, and from mourning into a good day: that they should make them days of feasting and joy, and of sending portions one to another, and gifts to the poor."*

EXHORTATION

It is not a pleasant thing to mourn. God does not want us to mourn but to celebrate and be joyous. Everyone looks forward to the day of their celebration. If you are single, you would look forward to celebrating your marriage and if you are married, your day of celebration would be the day you welcome your child to the world or their graduation ceremony. The list goes on and on. God desires that our lives be filled and enriched with divine celebration in every season and this is why we need to receive grace to celebrate.

As I would often say, getting married isn't a function of just beauty but a function of grace. It is expedient to pray and receive grace to celebrate. You need a divine enablement to celebrate as this world is characterized by wickedness and the evil ones would stop at nothing to abort the plan of God for your life. As you fast and wait upon the Lord in prayer, I see you receiving the grace to celebrate in Jesus name.

CONFESSION

Ecclesiastes 7:8a *"Better is the end of a thing than the beginning thereof."*

PRAYER POINT

1. My book of celebration open by fire in Jesus name.
2. My heaven of celebration open by fire in Jesus name.
3. My gates of celebration open by fire in Jesus name.
4. My season of celebration, manifest in Jesus name.
5. Those who will facilitate my celebration, appear in Jesus name.
6. Anointing to celebrate fall on me in Jesus

name.
7. Grace to celebrate locate me in Jesus name.
8. My opportunities for celebration manifest in Jesus name.
9. I enter my season of celebration in Jesus name.
10. May the wind of celebration blow upon me, my work and family in Jesus name.
11. Any embargo on my celebration is lifted in Jesus name.
12. Any power resisting my celebration, expire in Jesus name.
13. Any altar raised against my celebration shall scatter in Jesus name.
14. Battles against my celebration shall be defeated and dislodged in Jesus mighty name.
15. Angels of celebration, locate me and my family in Jesus name.

DAY 23

LORD GIVE ME A NEW EXPERIENCE

SCRIPTURE FOR THE DAY

Isaiah 43:18-19 *"Forget the former things; do not dwell on the past. See, I am doing a new thing! Now it springs up;*

do you not perceive it? I am making a way in the wilderness and streams in the wasteland."

EXHORTATION

When God wants to bring a man into a new experience, He instructs him on which way to go. It is expedient that you always go to God for instructions that are peculiar to you; no two instructions are the same and the instruction for tomorrow is not the same as that of today. He wants to lead you differently from the experiences of the generations before you. Let's take a walk down the scripture.

In the 12th chapter of Genesis, there was famine in the days of Abram before God changed his name to Abraham. Then he rose with his wife and went into Egypt. In Genesis 26, there was also a famine in the days of Abraham's son, Isaac. Isaac could have repeated the move of his father and gone to Egypt, but that would be wrong. Instead, God told Isaac to sojourn in Gerar despite the ravaging drought in that land. This instruction was different from the action of his father; the divine leading for his father was to move, while his was to stay. Even for the same set of circumstances, you cannot copy another's instructions and expect the same result. A new experience requires a new instruction.

There are areas God would love you to experience new dimensions:

· Your finance – (Psalm 37:25) and this can happen via God directing you into your new job, the new opening for your business, new opportunities to make money,

· Your health – (Mark 1:29) like Peter's mother-in-law you will enjoy instant healing,

· Your relationship – (Ruth 4:13) like Ruth; God will reorder your marital destiny,

· International exposure – (Acts 20:15) like it happened Paul, the Lord will open doors for you globally. Are you ready to experience new dimensions?

CONFESSION

Deuteronomy 8:7 *"For the LORD thy God bringeth thee into a good land, a land of brooks of water, of fountains and depths that spring out of valleys and hills;"*

PRAYER POINTS

1. Lord, send your light to lead me into a new experience of new dimension.
2. Lord, move me out of the queue of frustration and settle me in the land of fulfillment in Jesus' name.
3. Holy Ghost, terminate evil postponement of my testimonies like Rachel on the wedding day.
4. Conclusions of death and destruction against me backfire in Jesus' name.
5. Lord, bring me into a new experience in all areas of my life.
6. Power for new results, fall upon me now in Jesus' name.
7. Lord, take me out of the queue of life and from the crowd of no fulfillment.
8. Lord, disappoint every satanic appointment to kill me in the remaining days of this year.
9. Every evil altar erected against my moving forward into a new experience, I pull them down by fire in the name of Jesus.
10. I speak against the power of going in circles in my life; lose your hold over me in the name of Jesus.

11. Lord, renew my heart so that I can be ready for new dimensions in you.
12. Lord, help me leave behind the bitter times of the former days and move on to the better days ahead of me in Jesus name.
13. Lord, repair my broken ways and prepare me for new dimensions.
14. Lord, I choose to commit my decisions henceforth to you.
15. Lord, open my eyes and ears to receive new instructions from you.

DAY 24

LORD BLESS ME AND MY HOUSE

SCRIPTURE FOR THE DAY

2 Samuel 6:11 *"The ark of the LORD remained in the house of Obed-Edom the Gittite three months. And the LORD blessed Obed-Edom and all his household."* (NKJV)

EXHORTATION

The home is such a beautiful place that God love to intentionally pitch His tent. It is a place where our children are first taught to love God and learn of His ways. When a family thrives, the society and the world at large would thrive. The family might be the smallest unit in a society but its impact in the overall well being of a nation is deep. It is God's desire to see homes thrive in peace, safety, provision, the abundance of His love and presence.

This is why we would be praying for God's blessings upon our homes. Prayer changes things and whatever needs to be restored and put in place in your home, watch God step into those situations henceforth.

CONFESSION

Joshua 24:15b *"............But as for me and my house, we will serve the Lord."*

PRAYER POINTS

1. Lord, release the divine allocation for this family now.
2. Lord, we shall not repeat the mistake of our ancestors in this family.
3. Lord, give me grace to surpass the achievement of my predecessors.

4. Evil decree affecting my family be uprooted in the name of Jesus.
5. Let the progress of this family be released now.
6. What nobody ever achieved in my generation, this family must surpass it.
7. Lord, we release greatness into this family that will immortalize our family name in good time.
8. I cancel every attack over the education of all my children. (*Mention their names before the Lord*).
9. We forbid death, sickness and affliction in this family in Jesus name.
10. Lord, let your presence invade every corner and the life of every member of my household.
11. I declare that my house will be a home of peace in Jesus name.
12. May the fire and fervency of our altars not go cold but burn more and more.
13. Every member of my household will increase in the desire for the things of God in Jesus name.
14. May your love abound and more in our hearts in Jesus name.
15. For everyone in my house, I pray that we are kept in perfect peace.

DAY 25

THE HOLY SPIRIT

SCRIPTURE FOR THE DAY

Zechariah 4:6 *"Then he answered and spake unto me, saying, This is the word of the Lord unto Zerubbabel, saying, Not by might, nor by power, but by my spirit, saith the Lord of hosts."*

EXHORTATION

The Holy Spirit is the Spirit of God and the third person in trinity, although not different from God, the Father and God, the son - for God is mysteriously interwoven as one. The person of the Holy Spirit is widely misunderstood by many believers in the world today. The Holy Spirit plays different roles in the life of a believer. However, the first thing to understand is that the Holy Spirit is given to people who believe in Jesus to bind them together with God and help them become more like Him.

It is God who makes us stand firm in Christ. God anointed us, set His seal of ownership on us, and put His Spirit in our hearts as a deposit, guaranteeing what is to come. Throughout the Bible, the Holy Spirit equips people for ministry, gives people specific insight and wisdom, and teaches people how to interpret God's Word. In addition the Spirit communicates with the Father on people's behalf, and empowers Christians to live according to God's design.

Galatians 5:22-23 is a Bible verse that talks about the work of the Holy Spirit in the life of a believer. He gives people the skills and abilities they need to share God's love; these are sometimes called 'spiritual gifts.' God also testified to it by signs, wonders and various miracles, and by gifts of the Holy Spirit distributed according to His will. The Holy Spirit is unique and creative. The more you learn about Him, the easier it is to recognize His presence in your life.

CONFESSION

1 John 5:7 *"For there are three that bear witness in heaven: the Father, the Word, and the Holy Spirit; and these three are one."* (NKJV)

PRAYER POINTS

1. Father, thank you for the gift and promise of

the Holy Spirit.

2. Jesus the Baptizer with the Holy Spirit, fill me to overflow with your precious Holy Spirit, in Jesus name.
3. Lord, purify my heart by faith in the blood of Jesus to receive afresh baptism of the Holy Spirit.
4. Father Lord, baptize me with the Holy Ghost and fire as promised in your word in Jesus name.
5. Father visit my church with an outpouring of the Holy Spirit with accompanying signs in Jesus name.
6. Lord, shake our church and fellowship with a fresh outpouring of the Spirit in mighty signs and wonders, in Jesus name.
7. Lord, visit our church with the Spirit of grace and supplication resulting in revival, in Jesus name.
8. Father to re-ignite the gifts of the Holy Spirit in your life and that of your church, in Jesus name.
9. Lord, visit my family with deep convictions produced by the Holy Spirit so that every unsaved member of the family will be saved, in Jesus name.

10. Let the influence of the Holy Spirit be activated in my daily life.
11. Lord, let my actions be Spirit led and not be flesh led.
12. Oh Lord! Use me as a channel for the impartation of the Holy Spirit to many people who come my way.
13. Holy Spirit, find expression through me in Jesus name.
14. Holy Spirit, teach me your ways, Holy Spirit.
15. In the name of Jesus, my life shall bear the fruit of the Holy Spirit.

DAY 26

PRAYER FOR THE BODY OF CHRIST AND HCC WORLDWIDE

SCRIPTURE FOR THE DAY

1 Corinthians 12:27 *"Now you are the body of Christ, and members Individually."*

EXHORTATION

This is the season for the body of Christ to *"put on the whole armour of the Lord, the breastplate of righteousness, feet shod with the preparation of the gospel of peace. Above all, taking the shield of faith, wherewith we shall be able to quench all the fiery darts of the wicked and take the helmet of salvation, and the sword of the Spirit, which is the word of God."* (Eph. 6:13-17)

The devil's attack on the church can no longer be ignored. Christians are being attacked all over the world. There was a recent attack on innocent worshippers in Nigeria, West Africa, amongst other atrocities. It is a season to be sensitive as he continually fires arrows to the church causing competition, strife and division. Today, let us raise our voices in intercession for the body of Christ and all HCC churches planted worldwide, for the ever increasing glory of God and the pulling down of strongholds.

CONFESSION

Matthew 16:18 *"And I say unto thee, that thou art Peter, and upon this rock I will build my church and the gates of hell shall not prevail against it."*

PRAYER POINTS

1. Lord, let your purpose for each Christian establishment be fulfilled.
2. Every power fighting the Church of God shall

not prevail.

3. Lord, do not allow the devil to cause Christian leaders to do their will but yours.
4. We throw out the net of salvation to draw people from all over the world.
5. Let there be a fresh fire in the body of Christ and let the fire spread round the world.
6. Lord, send down the revival into our churches across nations.
7. Lord, usher Holyghost Christian Centre globally into a new dimension.
8. Lord purify the motive of your church and its leaders.
9. Lord, send us burden bearers to support the kingdom work financially.
10. Let new Chapters of Celebration be opened unto us in all HCC branches.
11. Every power fighting the body of Christ is subdued instantly in Jesus name.
12. In HCC Global, let the Lord increase us greatly.
13. We decree that the church will influence the world with the standards of heaven.
14. Let your Spirit be felt in all of our services O Lord.

15. Lord, fill our services with testimonies in Jesus name and draw men unto you because of the testimonies.

DAY 27

FRESH ANOINTING

SCRIPTURE FOR THE DAY

Acts 1:8 "*But ye shall receive power, after that the Holy Ghost is come upon you: and ye shall be witnesses unto me both in Jerusalem, and in all Judaea, and in Samaria, and unto the uttermost part of the earth.*"

EXHORTATION

Every believer in Christ should desire the supply of a fresh anointing, the anointing of yesterday is not sufficient for the task of today and tomorrow. The Bible tells us that the mercies of God are new every morning (Lamentations 3:22-23). In the same vein, the anointing of the Holy Spirit in us can be renewed on a regular basis.

What is the anointing? The anointing is the power of God in us; this power was given to us by the

Holy Spirit when we gave our hearts to Jesus, that is, when we became born again. This power in us must be stirred continually for maximum effectiveness. To stir up the anointing of God in us, and continually make it fresh, we must be given to continuous prayers. Paul said in the scriptures *"Give yourself continually to the ministry of the Word and Prayer."* (Acts6:4)

CONFESSION

Psalm 92:10 *"But my horn You have exalted like a wild ox; I have been anointed with fresh oil." (NKJV)*

PRAYER POINTS

1. O Lord, renew a right spirit within me and teach me to die to self.
2. Let the heavenly brush of the Lord scrub out all the dirtiness in my spiritual pipe, in Jesus name.
3. O Lord, ignite my calling with your fire.
4. O Lord, anoint me to pray without ceasing.
5. O Lord, establish me as a holy person unto you.
6. O Lord, restore my spiritual eyes and years.
7. O Lord, let the anointing to excel in my

spiritual and physical life fall on me.

8. O Lord, produce in me the power of self-control and gentleness.
9. Holy Ghost, breathe on me now, in the name of Jesus.
10. Holy Ghost fire, ignite me to the glory of God.
11. O Lord, let every rebellion flee from my heart.
12. I command every spiritual contamination in my life to receive cleansing by the blood of Jesus.
13. Every rusted spiritual pipe in my life, receive wholeness, in the name of Jesus.
14. I command every power, eating up my spiritual pipe to be roasted, in the name of Jesus.
15. I receive a brand new cloak of protection for covering by the Blood of Jesus.

DAY 28

LORD REVIVE AND FILL ME AFRESH

SCRIPTURE FOR THE DAY

Acts 2:1-5 *"There appeared unto them cloven tongues like as of fire, and it sat upon each of them. And they were all* *filled with the Holy Ghost, and began to speak with other tongues as the Spirit gave them utterance."*

EXHORTATION

Fresh fire simply means the anointing of the Holy Ghost burning ever afresh in your heart. It takes a Christian who is on fire to live like Christ Jesus. Every believer in Christ must always pray for fresh fire and fresh anointing. When a Christian is on fire, the devil cannot manipulate his life and blessings. A lot of Christians go from place to place for prayers, simply because they lack fire. When you carry fire, you become unstoppable and indestructible; it's like being fortified from within and a strong immunity against attacks.

One of the greatest weapons for crushing oppression is to be baptized with the fire of the Holy Ghost. The baptism of fire is the symbol of the overflowing presence of the Holy Spirit in your life. The moment you are endued with fire from on high, you will become master over circumstances and forces of darkness. This prayer programme will restore your lost glory and make you to declare that there is something in your life that can repel the enemy.

When you become baptized in the fire of the Holy Ghost, your life will become too hot for the enemy to handle. If you have noticed signs of oppression, intimidation, manipulation, and wickedness in your life, it is an indication of the fact that your fire has been extinguished. Rather than box shadows, you need to go back to the presence of God and receive fresh fire.

As you pray this prayer points for fresh fire, I see the oil of God upon your life being refreshed and rekindled in the name of Jesus.

CONFESSION

Psalm 138:7 *"Though I walk in the midst of trouble, You will revive me; You will stretch out Your hand Against the wrath of my enemies, And Your right hand will save me." (NKJV)*

PRAYER POINTS

1. Holy Ghost fire, envelope every area of my life, in the name of Jesus.
2. I receive fresh fire to run through the troops and leap over the wall in the name of Jesus.
3. My Father, arise with your fire of power and manifest your presence in my life, in the name

of Jesus.

4. Anything hindering the power of God in my life die in the name of Jesus.
5. I shall trample upon every serpent and scorpion of powerlessness in the name of Jesus.
6. Holy Ghost fire, incubate my ears, my eyes and my mouth in the name of Jesus.
7. Fire of excellence from heaven; begin to burn in every area of my life in the name of Jesus.
8. Every power failure, I sack you today in the name of Jesus.
9. Road blocks and obstacles to my flowing in your anointing clear them away, by fire in the name of Jesus.
10. My Father, arise for my help and turn me to an untouchable coal of fire in the name of Jesus.
11. Spirit of lukewarmness and procrastination in my life; I command you to die in the name of Jesus.
12. Father, let the Holy Spirit fill me afresh in the name of Jesus.
13. Father, let every fallow ground in my life be broken in the name of Jesus.
14. Father, incubate me with the Holy Ghost fire

in the name of Jesus.

15. Let every anti-power bondage break in my life in the name of Jesus.

DAY 29

REPOSITIONING FOR NEW DIMENSION

SCRIPTURE FOR THE DAY

Genesis 24:43-46 *"Behold, I stand by the well of water; and it shall come to pass, that when the virgin cometh forth to draw water, and I say to her, Give me, I pray thee, a little water of thy pitcher to drink; and she say to me, Both drink thou, and I will also draw for thy camels: let the same be the woman whom the Lord hath appointed out for my master's son. And before I had done speaking in mine heart, behold, Rebekah came forth with her pitcher on her shoulder; and she went down unto the well, and drew water: and I said unto her, Let me drink, I pray thee. And she made haste, and let down her pitcher from her shoulder, and said, ``Drink, and I will give thy camels drink also: so I drank, and she made the camels drink also".*

EXHORTATION

The story in the quoted text above was about Abraham's servant who found a wife for Isaac, being at the right place at the right time. The widow of Nain is also a very good illustration of how God orchestrates the steps of men to be at the right place at the right time (Luke 7:11-17). Here are certain truths about life;

1. You can either be at the right place at the wrong time,
2. Be at the wrong place at the right time,
3. Be at the wrong place at the wrong time, or
4. Be at the right place at the right time.

Being in the right place at the right time is orchestrated by God and it is the best. He sets up appointments in the right places and at the right time for those He loves. Ruth was at the right place at the right time when she found Boaz (Ruth 2:1-3). Success in life is a combination of passion, dedication, opportunities, hard work and being at the right place at the right time. If you want to be at the right place at the right time, the first step is to ask for the God of times and seasons to come into your life as your Lord and personal Saviour.

Ask for His cleansing power and forgiveness. It is after you have taken this first step that you are then entitled to enjoy the leading of the Holy Spirit.

CONFESSION:

Psalms 37:23 *"The steps of a good man are ordered by the Lord: and he delighteth in his way."*

PRAYER POINTS

1. Lord Jesus, I thank You for Your great love and mercy over my life.
2. I repent today for doing things my own way and neglecting your love and counsel.
3. Lord, my times and seasons are in Your hands; give me a new time and season of refreshing.
4. According to Psalms 37:23, order my steps to the right places as the year is ending
5. Let every invisible chain pulling my legs to the wrong places be destroyed in Jesus name.
6. I silence every strange voice calling me to go to the wrong place in Jesus name.
7. Every spell cast to manipulate my legs towards wrong places in life, be terminated in Jesus name.
8. Every power that wants to uproot me from the

house of bread and put me to the place of scarcity and suffering, die by fire in Jesus name.

9. O Lord by Your mercy, connect me to the right people in the right place in Jesus name.
10. I refuse to waste my life in the wilderness of confusion and college of ignorance in Jesus name.
11. Every evil covenant entered by my ancestors tying me down to a wrong place, be broken right now in Jesus name.
12. Abraham, Ruth and Mephibosheth, were delivered from wrong places; I shall also be delivered from any wrong place in Jesus name.
13. Every power targeted at my repositioning, catch fire in Jesus name.
14. Father let me walk in your timing in Jesus name.
15. Lord, upgrade my mind as you prepare me for repositioning in Jesus name.

DAY 30

STRENGTH TO ACCESS NEW DIMENSIONS

SCRIPTURE OF THE DAY

Isaiah 40:31 *"But they that wait upon the LORD shall renew their strength; they shall mount up with wings as eagles; they shall run, and not be weary; and they shall walk, and not faint."*

EXHORTATION

When the scripture says *"It is not by power nor by might but by the Spirit, says the Lord"*, they aren't just mere words, it is a fact! It further says that "*I can do all things through Christ that strengthens me*". This is to show that to access new dimensions in God; you have to be strengthened - not by your will power, technical know-how or your physical fitness but by God.

There is a dimension of strength that has sustained you to the level that you are at now. To attain a higher level, you need a higher dimension of strength, not only to attain the desired level but also to remain there. This is where the prayer of Paul for the Ephesians brethren becomes so crucial to all of us right now. It is a prayer you need to pray in faith at this time of the year (Ephesians 3:16). Here's what I have discovered; whenever God is taking someone to a new level, He first builds his character, tenacity, passion, faithfulness, integrity and drive. Then he proceeds to develop and strengthen him on his inside to fulfill God's purpose for his life.

Glory has weight. If you are going to carry a heavy weight of glory, then you must be strong inside to carry it without pressure, without cracking and without stumbling. At this crucial time of the year, you need to take some time aside to seek the face of God. He will visit and strengthen you for the next level.

CONFESSION

Psalm 68:35 *"O God, thou art terrible out of thy holy places: the God of Israel is he that giveth strength and power unto his people. Blessed be God."*

PRAYER POINTS

1. Give thanks to God because He is the One

who gives strength to His people.

2. Ask the Holy Spirit to clothe you with power, strength and might to move to the next level of God's plan for your life.
3. Ask the Lord to strengthen you with might in your inner man by the Holy Spirit.
4. New strength from on high fall upon me now in Jesus name.
5. Lord renew my strength to stand against hindrances to next year's success.
6. Resurrection power, fall on me in Jesus name.
7. Oh Lord, by your Holy Spirit; renew my strength and restore my effectiveness in Jesus name.
8. Anywhere my life is leaking out the blessings of God; I seal it up by the blood of Jesus.
9. Empty me, Oh Lord, of all corruption and vanity and fill me with glory and honour in Jesus name.
10. Purge my heart, O Lord, of all traces of worldliness and idolatry in Jesus name.
11. Renew my strength O Lord, to serve you faithfully to the end in Jesus name.
12. Soak me O Lord, with your end-time latter-rain in Jesus name.

13. Lord, help me to rely on you for strength at all times in Jesus name.
14. On days when I am weak, teach me to always rely on your strength in Jesus name.
15. I receive the strength of body, strength of mind and strength of soul in Jesus name.

Author's Contact

Mainland Office:
Solution Arena, 156, Ikorodu Road
Onipanu Bus Stop, Lagos.

Island Office:
Testimony Place, Plot 5, Akiogun Road,
Oniru New Market, Lekki, Lagos.

email:
amosfenwa@hccworld.org,
president@amosfenwaministry.org

website:
www.hccworld.org,
www.amosfenwaministry.org

phone:
+234 (0) 812 511 3314,
+234 (0) 803 338 7124,
+234 (0) 703 727 6477

DIRECTORY

HCC GLOBAL OFFICE
Solution Arena
156, Ikorodu Road
Onipanu Bus Stop, Lagos.
Tel: +2348033004930,
www.hccworld.org
Email: tunderichard@hccworld.org
Central Administrator: TUNDE RICHARD

LAGOS HEADQUARTER
Solution Arena
156, Ikorodu Road
Onipanu Bus Stop, Lagos.
Tel: +2348023097589, +2348063037717
www.hccworld.org
Email: adedeji697@gmail.com
Pastor-in-charge: EMMANUEL ADEDEJI

OGBOMOSO, OYO STATE
House of Mercy
Behind Ori-Oke Community High School,
Odo- Alamo, Ogbomoso,
Oyo State.
Tel: +2348033704031, +2348076016687,
+2348073045600
fenwadeborah@yahoo.com
Pastor-in-charge: MOSES FENWA

APO, FEDERAL CAPITAL, ABUJA
Home of Achievers
Plot 211, Cadastral Zone B14,
Along Apo Mechanic Village road,
Before Shoprite, Dutse District, Abuja
Tel: +2348023189362, +2348076016672,
+2348137031889
Email: hgccabuja@yahoo.com
ZONAL PASTOR: DR AYO TEGBE

IKEJA, LAGOS STATE
Royal Family
OLOKUN AYO HOUSE
15 KudiratAbiola Way,
Middle Floor,
Ojota Bus Stop, Ikeja, Lagos.
Tel: +2347058770510
Pastor-in-charge: TAIWO OMOJOLA

LUGBE,FEDERAL CAPITAL TERRITORY, ABUJA
Home of Grace
1st Avenue,
FHA Lugbe,
Behind Royal Rainbow School,
FCT, Abuja.
Tel: +2348100587775, +2348173297803
Email: hcclugbe@yahoo.com
Pastor-in-charge: EZEKIEL FENWA

EGBEDA-AKOWONJO, LAGOS STATE
Glory House
46 Akowonjo Rd,
Bakery Bus Stop,Egbeda,
Lagos.
Tel:+234 8104910929, +234 8170236050
babsdy84@gmail.com
Pastor-in-charge: ADEJORO BABALOLA

LONDON, UNITED KINGDOM
The Elevation Point
The Elevation Point Building,
3, Herringham Road,
Thames Wharf Barrier Charlton,
London SE7 8NJ
By Charlton Car Wash
Tel: +447961480394
Email:info@hgcc.org.uk
Pastor-in-charge: OLUMIDE ADEYILEKA

NEW JERSEY, UNITED STATES
House of Stars; Place of Refuge
1323 Burnet Avenue Union Township NJ 07083 USA
Tel: +862-849-6644, 973-731-1495, Fax: +973-483-3825
Email: hgpcim@yahoo.com
ZONAL PASTOR: DR JOSEPH SIJU

LEKKI, LAGOS STATE,
Testimony Place
Plot 5, Akiogun Road, by Oniru Market Road,
(Alternative Route A, After Lekki Toll Gate)
Lekki, Lagos.
Tel:+2348161681593
Email: info@hcclekki.org
Pastor-in-charge: FEMI OKANLAWON

KUJE, FEDERAL CAPITAL TERRITORY, ABUJA
Home of Overcomers
Beside Home Connections,
Tipper Garage,
Off Airport road,
Kuje, FCT.
+2347081008060, +2348076016672
Email: hcckuje@yahoo.com
Minister-in-charge: SHOLA ENIOLA

ATLANTA, UNITED STATES
House of Restoration
2260 FellowshipRoad, Tucker GA 30084
(Behind NAPA Building)
Off Lawrenceville Hwy,
Tel: +1 848 236 6044, +1 706 300 2322, +1 862 849 6644
Email: hccatlanta2@gmail.com
Pastor-in-charge: DAVID ALABI OBAFEMI

HOUSTON, UNITED STATES
HCC Light House
6981 S Texas 6, Houston, TX 77083
Right next to Chez Michelle Restaurant
Contact: +1 (862) 849 6644, +1 (281) 906 7327
Email: lighthouse@hcc.org
Pastor-in-charge: JAMES CHINEDU

KUBWA, FEDERAL CAPITAL TERRITORY, ABUJA
Home of Abundance
Okitipupa Crescent,
Opposite MTN Office,
Off Nadrem Supermarket,
Phase 4, Kubwa, FCT Abuja.
Tel: +2348037052702, + 2348079367664
Email: solomonakuboh@gmail.com
Minister-in-charge: SOLOMON B. AKUBOH

NEWSPRING CHURCH
(HCC Youth Expression)
69, MurtalaMohhamed Way,
Yaba, Lagos.
Tel: + 2348028398692, + 2348028117178,
Email: davidbankole73@gmail.com
Minister-in-charge: DAVID BANKOLE

SOUTH JERSEY, UNITED STATES
Jubilee Place
Timber Creek Apartments
1801 Laurel Road, Lindenwold,
NJ 08021, USA
Tel: +1 862452 4458,
Email: hccjubileeplace@gmail.com
Pastor-in-charge: SEYI OLANREWAJU

OTHER BOOKS BY THE AUTHOR

HOW TO ENJOY
NOT ENDURE YOUR
MARRIAGE
AMOS FENWA

SINGLES'
CHECKLIST
• The Syllabus Has Changed •
AMOS FENWA

25
UNAVOIDABLE
THINGS
TO DISCUSS
BEFORE
YOU SAY
I DO
AMOS FENWA

AMOS FENWA
The Man and the Woman
OVER 77 FACTS ABOUT OPPOSITE SEX THAT MAKES YOU ATTRACTIVE
CARE TO DARE
AMOS FENWA
Amos Fenwa
How to Set A New Family Record

Parenting
WITH
Ease
21ST CENTURY SOLUTIONS
TO NEW CHALLENGES
AMOS FENWA

GOD'S MERCY HOW TO OBTAIN IT
AMOS FENWA
GOD'S
MERCY
HOW TO
OBTAIN IT
AMOS FENWA

My HANDS Are
Blessed
Not CURSED
MY HANDS ARE BLESSED NOT CURSED
AMOS FENWA

www.ingramcontent.com/pod-product-compliance
Lightning Source LLC
La Vergne TN
LVHW010600160826
845677LV00013B/3195

* 9 7 8 9 7 8 7 9 1 1 0 1 3 *